The Life Worth Living

G. RAYMOND CARLSON
Adapted from *Gospel of John* by Stanley M. Horton

RadíantBOOKS

Gospel Publishing House/Springfield, Mo. 65802

02-0876

THE LIFE WORTH LIVING
© 1975 by the Gospel Publishing House
Springfield, Missouri 65802
Adapted from *Gospel of John* by Stanley M. Horton
© by the Gospel Publishing House
Library of Congress Catalog Number: 75-22607
ISBN 0-88243-876-X
Printed in the United States of America

**A teacher's guide for individual or group study
with this book is available from the
Gospel Publishing House (order number 32-0160;
ISBN 0-88243-160-9).**

Contents

The Life Worth Living

CHAPTER 1/Read John 1 and 2

Have you heard about the millionaire who so loved his car that he asked to be buried in it? Upon his death, the mortuary prepared a sufficiently large grave dressed the man in his sharpest sport coat, sat him behind the wheel, put a cigar in his mouth, and set the speedometer at 65 miles an hour. A well-meaning, sport-loving friend at the funeral said, "Man, that's living!" But nothing could have been deader. The make-believe episode offers a commentary on how some people view life and what or who is viewed as Lord of life.

The Gospel of John was written that we might know how to have life (John 20:30,31) through Jesus the Lifegiver. The introduction to the Gospel (John 1:1-18) projects the theme by declaring that God came to earth in the Person of His Son, born at Bethlehem, to live among men. Full of grace and truth, He forever involved himself in our human problems, that He might show us how to really live.

OF THUNDER AND LOVE

Three key words—life, light, love—are noted in the Gospel. John, the writer of the Gospel, had been known as one of the sons of thunder (Mark 3:17). He and his brother James had possessed natures which made them ready to call down lightning and thunder.

A change came to John. He became known as the apostle of love. Once the son of thunder, now the example of love. What happened? The answer is simple. He had received new life through the Giver of life, the Living Word. And that spark of divine life expanded into a consuming flame to burn out self and make John like Jesus.

John enjoyed this life, walked in this light, absorbed the warmth of this love as he followed Jesus. That same experience can be ours as we follow Him.

Jesus' purpose in history is an eternal and perfect plan of redemption. It goes far beyond the highest perfection of the systems of men. It transcends our fondest hopes and dreams because it began in and continues for eternity. That purpose was not fulfilled through Jesus' perfect life on earth. It came to fruition through the Cross and Resurrection.

Sin is at the root of our problems. It is the culprit in all that hurts and destroys. It lurks behind every tragedy. Its wages is death. War, poverty, injustice, spring from that common root. Jesus came to deal with the root problem of human misery, and He conquered it once and for all by His death at Calvary. The empty tomb shouts the victory for everyone who believes.

We cannot solve our problems by dealing only with the symptoms. We need to go deeper. Jesus dealt with the causes in the lives He changed. And He begins with causes when He changes us.

The most respected, most widely discussed, most optimistic message this world has ever received is the account of the claims of Jesus Christ for himself. This book about the Gospel of John will discuss some of those claims and the provision of life, light, and love made by Jesus. Will you join us on a journey with Jesus through the Gospel of John?

MEET THE LIFEGIVER

The Gospel of John begins with eight majestic statements:

1. *In the beginning was the Word* (John 1:1). Jesus is co-eternal with God.

2. *The Word was with God* (John 1:1). Jesus is co-existent with God.

3. *The Word was God* (John 1:1). Jesus is co-equal with God.

4. *The Word was made flesh* (John 1:14). He is God incarnate, God clothed in human flesh.

5. *The Word dwelt among us* (John 1:14). Jesus is uniquely Christ, the Son of God and Son of Man.

6. *No man hath seen God at any time* (John 1:18). We can't see God with our natural eyes. He is invisible, but He *is!*

7. *We beheld His glory* (John 1:14). The invisible became visible.

8. *The only begotten Son, which is in the bosom of the Father, he hath declared him* (John 1:18). Jesus became the full revelation of the Father (John 14:9).

WHERE DID IT ALL START?

Every thoughtful person asks himself some important questions. Where did everything begin? How did everything begin? There is only one logical answer—an eternal uncaused First Cause. There is no alternative. The Bible teaches that this uncaused First

Cause was the eternal God, existing eternally as Father, Son, and Holy Spirit.

Before the Beginning

Christ is eternal. Genesis opens with the statement, "In the beginning God created the heaven and the earth." But John goes back even farther, back before there was a material creation. The Gospel opens with "In the beginning was the Word." Before things began, the Living Word already *was*. We can't comprehend eternity with our finite minds. But thank God we can take the leap of faith.

Christ is divine. In the Godhead He was a distinct person; He was "with" God. In His nature, however, He was God. Described as the Word, Jesus Christ is the full and accurate expression of the mind of God. The statement, "the Word was God," lays the foundation for the startling claims that follow in this Gospel.

A chaplain stood before a company of weary soldiers who had just returned from the front. He saw them discouraged, exhausted, absolutely beat. A steady drizzle drenched their fatigues as they stood in an open field to hear the Word.

"My text," the chaplain began, "is 'What think ye of Christ?'"

He paused and then went on, "My sermon is 'What think ye of Christ?'"

Then he shouted, "Company dismissed!"

That was great preaching. It struck home to the hearts of these men who had so recently faced death. The greatest question you will ever answer is "What think ye of Christ?" Dull men, shallow men, argue over Christ's deity. Really intelligent men recognize

His divinity. They don't argue it, they believe. Chesterton expressed it:

> There was a man who dwelt in the east centuries ago,
> And now I cannot look at a sheep or a sparrow,
> A lily or a cornfield, a raven or a sunset,
> A vineyard or a mountain, without thinking of Him.
> If this is not divine, what is?

Christ shared in the creation. "He created everything there is—nothing exists that He didn't make" (John 1:3, *The Living Bible Paraphrased*). Only God, the Trinity, is uncreated. And the greatness of Christ is shown in the fact that He is the Creator of all things. "He was before all else began and it is His power that holds everything together" (Colossians 1:17, *The Living Bible Paraphrased*).

Christ became God in human flesh. He was eternally God. But He became a man at a point in time. This is called the incarnation.

THE ULTIMATE IN REVELATION

The incarnation teaches us many lessons. It shows us something of the capacities and limitations of human flesh. Christ submitted to the limitations of human flesh "and yet without sin."

God in Christ chose to identify with us in a human body, subject to the problems and temptations of human nature. He is forever involved with our needs because He chose to be. God is not a God off somewhere trying to understand our human experiences. In the Person of Christ, He tasted the trials of everyday life—weariness, injustice, temptation, sorrow, hunger, thirst, heartache, tragedy, failure of friends, cruelty of enemies. Because He came, He understands; He knows how we feel. There is no human experience we encounter that He can't share with us.

Christ, the One who is the Word of God and the

Light and Life of men, came to the world. Due to the perversity of sin, most people did not recognize Him. But those who received Him knew His glory as they saw, heard, and touched Him.

"As many as received him, to them gave he power to become the sons of God, even to them that believe on his name: which were born, not of blood, nor of the will of the flesh, nor of the will of man, but of God" (John 1:12,13). These are bold, jolting words for the seeking person. They are the promise of God as He invades time and history and draws men to himself. God calls, but He will not force himself on us. We must sense our staggering need, and confess it, and accept the complete answer from God. The formula seems simple enough on the surface. But it is crushing to our ego, for it involves the complete surrender of our wills to His. This is the price of God's free gift.

Christ came to reveal God (John 1:18). God is Spirit (John 4:24) and so is invisible. Jesus revealed Him in visible, human form. And when He came to reveal God, He also came to redeem us.

This is the ultimate in revelation. No other form of revelation could have been as effective. Once the Word put on shoes and walked, no other disclosure would ever be needed. He "dwelt," literally "pitched a tent," among men. The Word that "was made flesh" characterized grace and truth (John 1:14). Grace and truth came by Him (John 1:17). Grace is the unearned, unmerited favor of God. Truth is reality as opposed to the symbolism of the Old Testament law which was given by Moses. The Law was the shadow of things to come. Christ brought the good things the Law could only promise.

A dirty, disorderly room may not appear to be such

when dimly lighted. But once the full rays of bright sunshine dispel its shadows, the true situation is revealed. The coming of Christ, the Light of the world, brought into boldest relief the utter desolation of man's lostness. But He also brought love and life. The purpose of the Holy Spirit in giving us the Gospel of John is that we might believe, and by believing have life (John 20:31).

BEHOLD THE LAMB

Lambs were a familiar sight in Jesus' day. Flocks of sheep were to be found everywhere. In fact it was not uncommon for a household to include an orphan lamb that slept with the family at night.

But John the Baptist in announcing Jesus as the "Lamb of God" (John 1:29,36) had something far greater in mind than a literal lamb. What did he mean? The Old Testament gives a threefold answer.

1. *The Passover Lamb.* Of all events in Israel's history, none was of greater importance than the Exodus from Egypt. They looked back to this time as the beginning of their national life. When the Israelites prepared to leave Egypt, God delivered them from the judgment that fell on Egypt's firstborn through the sprinkled blood of the Passover lamb. The Jews still commemorate this deliverance by eating the Passover lamb. The importance of the blood of that lamb was kept before them. Paul writes, "For even Christ our passover is sacrificed for us" (1 Corinthians 5:7).

2. *The Daily Lamb.* Twice daily, at 9 in the morning and 3 in the afternoon, the Israelites offered a lamb on the altar of sacrifice (Numbers 28:4). These were also the regular hours of prayer (Acts 3:1;

10:3,30). Christ is not only God's Lamb given to take away the sin of the world. He is also the Lamb who makes possible our daily communion with the Father.

In John 1:29 John the Baptist presented Christ to the multitudes at Bethabara as the Lamb who came to take away sin. In verse 36 he again announced Him as the Lamb, this time to his own followers, as the Lamb who provides communion. As we look to the Lamb of God, first for forgiveness and then for fellowship, we become conformed to His image.

3. *The Suffering Lamb.* Christ is also pictured in Scripture as the suffering Lamb (Isaiah 53:5-7, 10-12) who died as the sacrifice for our sins (1 Peter 1:18,19).

THE BAPTIZER IN THE SPIRIT

John recognized that he could not take away the sins of the people. He could not even handle his own. The Lamb of God alone could forgive sins. John could not help others to live a life pleasing to God any more than he could make his own life conformable to God's standards. It would take the Holy Spirit to do that. John had been told to look for the coming Baptizer, and he recognized Jesus as the One when the Spirit descended upon Him as a dove on the occasion of His baptism in water (John 1:32,33).

A SERIES OF FIRSTS

The first *witness* to Christ in the Gospel of John was John the Baptist (John 1:29-36). The first *disciples* were Andrew, Peter, Philip, and Nathanael. They became the first *soul winners*. Andrew brought Peter to Jesus, and Philip introduced Nathanael (John 1:37-51). Chapter 2 records the first *miracle* (John 2:9-11) and the first *conflict* (John 2:15-19).

Jesus entered His public ministry by going to a wedding as an invited guest. When you prepare your wedding invitation list, put His name at the top. Jesus is not welcome at many weddings. He would feel terribly out of place. A wedding isn't really a Christian wedding unless both parties are Christians and are committed to establishing a Christian home.

The fact that "this beginning of his signs" (the miracle of turning water into wine) was given at a wedding has some things to say to us. Divine approval rests upon innocent festivity and pleasure. The Lord has an interest in human affairs. He wanted to be at the wedding. He wants to share our joy at a time of gladness.

Jesus didn't absent himself from the place of sorrow either. He interrupted funerals and emptied tombs. He wept with those who mourned. But neither did He stay away from the place of joy. He is not only with us in times of crisis and grief. Jesus was a social creature, and He loved a good time. He was no killjoy. His presence at the wedding didn't distract from the festivities, for He contributed to the occasion as only He could.

The Lord's presence at the wedding indicates He wants to sanctify the home at its beginning. True, He can salvage a home on the verge of dissolution; but, if you invite Him into your marriage at the very beginning, you can save a lot of heartache.

SHARING IN A MIRACLE

Jesus performed the miracle, yet He gave several people the joy of sharing in it. Mary shared by informing Jesus of the host's predicament. She didn't presume to tell Him what to do. She just called the problem to His attention and left it with Him. What a lesson for us!

The servants shared by obeying His command and doing a seemingly foolish thing. That was obedience! They filled the waterpots with water. The next step called for faith. They dipped out "the water that was now wine" and brought it to the master of ceremonies. Obedience and faith move the hands of God. "To obey is better than sacrifice" (1 Samuel 15:22). "And his disciples believed on him" (John 2:11).

REAL LIFE GETS BETTER

The way of the world is to give its best first, and then leave the deceived dupe to drink the bitter dregs of disappointment and disillusionment. But with Jesus the Lifegiver it is different. The miracle—water into wine—illustrates the way of the Christian life. Jesus saves the best for the last.

Childhood is marked by carefree days and endless wonder. Romantic youth is idealistic, visionary, optimistic. Responsible adulthood features maturity, love, achievement. The golden years are meant for wisdom, fond memories, gracious sweetness. Like the sunset, they can be the most beautiful time of life's full day for the child of God. As the sun sinks behind the horizon, we are ushered to the glory to awaken in the brightness of our Lord's face. Life can be richer, fuller and sweeter from day to day if it is lived in Christ. He keeps the "best for the last!" (John 2:10, *The Living Bible Paraphrased*).

As Jesus changed the water into wine, so He can change your heart and life and destiny. And then at

14

the end of the corridor of life, the door will open to the heavenly home.

The story of the Lord's first miracle illustrates how full obedience brings full blessing. The servants filled the waterpots brimful with water. The result was that these pots were soon brimful of wine. The measure of their obedience was the measure of their reward. Had they half filled them with water, they would have ended with the pots being half filled with wine.

The Lord's compensations are always in accord with our response to His known will. He alone can perform the miracle. But we have our part to do. We must fill the waterpots with water.

What Jesus told the servants to do seemed rather silly, but they obeyed, and the result was a supply of better wine than they had been serving. The family escaped embarrassment; the shadow threatening the festivities passed.

"Whatsoever he saith unto you, do it" (John 2:5). We need to obey the Word of the Lord. But to obey His Word we first need to know it. That means we must faithfully study our Bibles. But more is needed. We must be "doers of the Word, and not hearers only."

What Do You Mean—
Born Again?

CHAPTER 2/Read John 3

Someone (maybe a preacher—they do things like that) observed that the Bible contains three fundamental 3rd chapters which are basic to the understanding of the gospel. They are the 3rd of Genesis, the 3rd of Romans and the 3rd of John. In the first we have ruin; in the second, redemption; in the third, regeneration. Our ruin came by the Fall in the Garden of Eden. Our redemption came by the shed blood of Calvary. Our regeneration comes by the Holy Spirit.

The 3rd chapter of John records one of the greatest interviews of all time. People were always approaching Jesus for interviews. And He didn't have an advance man making arrangements. Nor did He plant anyone in the audience to stage the questions and perimeters. Jesus took on all comers and fielded every question. Observing His methods can afford one of the best lessons possible on the art of teaching.

John records two interviews in chapters 3 and 4. And what a difference in the interviewees! In this chapter the chap is a Jewish religious leader. In John 4 it's an unhappy woman with an immoral background. Study them together to get the picture—the dignified theologian over against the first century swinger.

They had one thing in common—great big searching questions. Both were dissatisfied and fed up! Nicodemus, the religious leader, was bewildered; the woman, a member of a despised race, was sick of it all. And Jesus met them both, totally satisfying their deepest longings.

Now Nicodemus came to Jesus after dark. Just why we don't know. Some have accused him of fearing the ridicule of the crowd, but that's doubtful. The important thing is that he came. And he came with an unprejudiced mind.

That visit at night brought two teachers together. The one was a blind, groping seeker after truth and light; the other was the Truth and the Light who came to open blind eyes. The first one came from among men, the latter from God. At first they met face-to-face (vv. 2 and 3). Then it was mind to mind (vv. 4 to 8), and before long they enjoyed heart to heart fellowship (vv. 9-21).

AIN'T NEVER BEEN BORNED

Someone asked an ignorant young girl, "Topsy, how old are you?" "Dunno." "Well, when were you born?" "I ain't never been borned; I just growed up." That fits too many church members. They just ain't never been born—born again, that is. They just "growed up," just grew up in the church.

Now that's what Jesus was telling Nicodemus. He needed to be born again. For nearly 2,000 years people have in turn been irritated, amused, indifferent to Jesus' command, "You must be born again."

If these words of Jesus confuse you, you're not alone. They confused Nicodemus at first. He had a mind's eye picture of going through the maternity ward again. That just didn't make much sense. And I guess he wasn't too anxious for that experience.

But Jesus was talking about a spiritual birth. And don't ever forget it. It's a *birth* and not a reformation. And it's not just a figure of speech. You can get properly related to God through personal faith in Jesus Christ. That's the new birth. That's what takes Christianity out of the just-another-religion category. If God didn't do something to the believer's spirit, then Christianity would have a hollow ring. You and I need something beyond our feeble efforts of reform. We need God's gift of life through the new birth to give us real life.

You and I—and all men—need the experience of the new birth. Nicodemus needed to be born again despite his many religious, social, and economic advantages. Look at this man to whom Jesus said, "You must be born again!"

WHAT REALLY COUNTS

Nicodemus was *religious.* He was a member of the "church." He was a religious leader, a member of the Sanhedrin, the supreme council of the Jewish people. But Jesus declared, "You must be born again!"

Nicodemus *knew the Scriptures.* He was orthodox in doctrine and flawless in practice, faithful in the observance of the Sabbath and the payment of tithes. But Jesus said, "You must be born again!"

Nicodemus was *sincere.* If not, Jesus would have rebuked him, for the Lord hates hypocrisy. Yet Jesus stated, "You must be born again!"

Nicodemus was *morally upright.* Are you one of those who defines your religion by "do's" and "don'ts"? You ask some people what Christianity or their church belief is and they reply, "We don't smoke . . . don't drink . . . and on." Jesus didn't tell Nico-

18

demus to quit cursing . . . stealing . . . getting drunk. The Lord didn't tell him to pay tithes, to observe the Sabbath, to keep his marriage vows. It appears Nicodemus was upright, but Jesus told him, "You must be born again!"

Nicodemus was *cultured, refined, decent, honorable, educated, financially successful,* but none of these was sufficient. He needed to be born again. And so must we.

HATCHED AGAIN

Someone—no doubt, a keen observer—said, "Some men needed to be hatched again and hatched different." And I believe all of us—butcher, baker, candlestick maker—need to be "hatched" again.

LIFE'S GREAT QUESTION

"What think ye of Christ?" is the greatest question you will ever answer. Your answer will determine your eternal destiny. You and I—and all men—will face God at His judgment bar. We don't determine the time and place, or whether or not it shall occur. God does that (Hebrews 9:27).

We can determine how we'll stand before God. We can come either as forgiven sinners or be judged for sin at the great white throne and end in eternal perdition (Revelation 20:11-15).

Two men filed wills, one in the 16th century, the other early in the 20th century. The one whose will was dated in May 1674 was a minister whose worldly goods amounted to some books, a few relics of furniture, and about $32 of other valuables.

This will read in part: " With my whole soul, I embrace the mercy which He has exercised to me through Jesus Christ, atoning for my sins by the merits of His death and passion, that in this way He might satisfy for all my crimes and faults, and blot them from His remembrance . . . that under His shadow I may be able to stand at the Judgment Seat."

The other testator of the second will was one of America's richest men at the time of his death.

His will stated: "I commit my soul into the hands of my Saviour in full confidence that, having redeemed it and washed it in His most precious blood, He will present it faultless before my heavenly Father, and I entreat my children to maintain the blessed doctrine of the complete Atonement for sin through the blood of Jesus Christ."

The first man was John Calvin, the famous French theologian from Geneva, Switzerland. The second man was J. Pierpont Morgan, renowned banker and financier of the early part of this century.

Though different in many ways, Calvin and Morgan were both alike in their trust in Christ. John Calvin didn't plead his leadership as a theologian, nor his poverty. J. P. Morgan did not plead his riches, nor his philanthropy. Both men claimed the merits of Christ's redemptive work at Calvary. And that was found by believing "You must be born again!" That's what really counts!

Without the new birth, neither Nicodemus, Calvin, Morgan, you nor I can see, understand, or even glimpse the kingdo mof God—to say nothing of entering it. None of us have a spark of divinity just waiting to be fanned into a flame. Try to fan it and you'll find no holy flame. The new birth is absolutely essential. We must receive a new life and a new nature which is not our own, but which comes to us from outside us, from above.

The possibility of receiving a new nature comes as God's gift of love. God's love is always self-giving.

That was the question a woman put to her pastor, a question he was hard put to answer. His preaching was devoid of the very heart and core of the gospel. As Martin Luther said, John 3:16 is "the Bible in a nutshell."

Have we become too familiar with the words of John 3:16? Thousands of us quote them from memory; they fall easily from our lips. Have we really plumbed their depths?

The most beautiful description of love which has ever entered the human mind is given in this brief verse of 25 words. The message is profound, but the words are simple. Nearly all the words are monosyllables—God, love, world, gave, Son, life.

"God so loved the world." That's love with definition. That's love as wide as eternity. God's love is more than emotion; it's an energy. It's more than sentiment; it's service.

"That He gave." God's love is expressive in its action. Real love must have self expression; it must *do* something to and for the object of love. True love is driven to action. Christ gave Himself *to* the world in His Incarnation and *for* the world on the Cross.

God's love is beautiful in its choice. "God so loved the *world."* Not mountains, plains, oceans; not animals, birds and fish; not trees, flowers, fruit, vegetation; God loved you and me and all men.

"His only begotten Son." God's Son was the jewel of heaven, the theme song of angels, the most precious gift available. Cutting through the jungle growth of human waywardness, God Himself appeared to reclaim what had been lost. The Son of God was born the virgin's Son. He came, not with a display of pomp and power, but as the lowly Child cushioned on hay

in a donkey motel. In a world of sickness and sorrow, poverty and want, of filthy streets and broken homes He climbed a bleak hill with a rough, wooden crossbeam on His back. Crucified to death between two wretched thieves, He found a resting place in a tomb prepared for another's lifeless body.

That was not the end; it was the beginning. Christ broke the hold of death to proclaim peace and pardon to *whosoever*. *Whosoever* is a word with my name on it. It is spelled with *your* name as well. There is no limit to the extent of His love.

To All, Yet Selective

Believeth. The offer is extensive, but the actual bestowment is selective. The offer can be effective only for those who believe. Love is fulfilled only as it is returned. "Whosoever believeth" is the only key to open heaven's door.

Shall not perish. Perish—what a hopeless word! Only six letters, and in those two syllables are gathered all the sorrows of humanity, all the twisted hopes of the race, all the terror and agony of hell, the lostness of an eternity without God.

Hopeless or Hope?

Life on this planet is subject to change, decay, death. James pointedly asks, "What is your life?" (James 4:14). And the answer comes back stark and cold, "It is even a vapour that appeareth for a little time, and then vanisheth away." Bertrand Russell gloomily stated, "The life of man is a long march through the night, surrounded by invisible foes, tortured by weariness and pain, toward a goal that few can hope to reach and where none can tarry long."

You Can Beat the Rap

Everlasting life. Life can be wonderful. The living Christ offers new life, eternal life. That is the eternal benefit of God's love. God, in His love, has provided our redemption from perishing. And God's gift is life, everlasting life.

God's love was revealed to us at Calvary. Drop the Cross from our preaching and you have drained the life blood from the gospel. What have we left? Ethics without energy, principles without power, human struggling without divine enabling. The love of Jesus at Calvary took your sins, and mine, and suffered over them. From His bleeding body and broken heart flowed the free grace of God to forgive our feverish ways, cleanse the uncleanness of soul, and beautify our graceless life with the loveliness of His own spirit, mind and nature.

Can you conceive anything greater than God's love? The highest reach of His love is in its self-sacrifice. He gave life itself, and that life was in the blood. From the bosom of God to the inglorious death of the Cross. Shame beyond description. Yet out of that great gift of love came a perfect remedy for sin.

Are You Saved?

Believe and you are saved (John 3:17). The word *saved* is often ignored and even avoided by many. Salvation is God's work; you are saved on account of Jesus Christ. *Salvation* is a wonderful word, as important as *creation*. Actually, salvation is bigger; it involves far more! God is the Creator, and He is also the Saviour. When He effected salvation, He did something as great as creation. Heaven and earth shall pass away (Mark 13:31), but His second creation (Ephesians 2:10), the saved, have eternal life. This is not a big, complicated matter. The Bible declares clearly, "He that hath the Son hath life; and he that hath not the Son of God hath not life" (1 John 5:12).

Do You Have Photophobia?

"Men loved darkness rather than light" (John 3:19). When a patient in an ophthalmic (that's a $64 word for something about eye trouble) hospital prefers darkness rather than the brightness of the sun, the doctors call it photophobia. Photophobia is an indication of a serious eye disease. Sufferers with these symptoms huddle in the dark, bury their faces, avoid the light.

Spiritual photophobia afflicts those whose deeds are evil (John 3:19). "They hated the heavenly Light because they wanted to sin in the darkness. They stayed away from that Light for fear their sins would be exposed and they would be punished. But those doing right come gladly to the Light to let everyone see that they are doing what God wants them to (John 3:20,21, *The Living Bible Paraphrased*).

Jesus' encounter with Nicodemus was in the realm of light and darkness. Nicodemus steps from the scene to reappear in chapter 7 of the Gospel. The last time we see him (John 19:39) is after Jesus' death. He joined with Joseph of Arimathaea in preparing Jesus' body for burial. He who first came to Jesus by night came out in the open when the night of death fell upon Jesus. When the cause seemed lost and open discipleship was dangerous, he took a public stand for Christ. What is your stand?

A Liberated Woman

CHAPTER 3/Read John 4 and 5

How would you like to be on an investigating committee? Apparently some people in Washington do. Seems they feel they're doing their thing, especially if they can get on camera and see their names in the headlines.

What if you'd been on a committee to check out the qualifications of witnesses for our Lord? How would you have reacted if a woman, who by her own admission was living immorally, sought to become a disciple? And what if she belonged to a group that had nothing to do with *your* group?

Just such a picture, another momentous interview, is graphically painted in chapter 4 of the Gospel. A woman was walking across a field alone, out of sorts with everybody. She had tried five husbands and forsaken them all. Now she was living out of wedlock with another.

She is a total contrast to Nicodemus—the religious moralist who kept the law meticulously. He was a Jew; she, a Samaritan. Society highly respected him; she was an outcast. He was morally perfect; she had lost her virtue. He was wealthy, cultured, educated; she was poor, ignorant, illiterate. He sought Jesus to inquire; she met Jesus as a foreigner. Yet despite their differences, both had the same need of spiritual transformation.

ARE YOU LISTENING?

Everybody wants someone to talk to, someone to listen. Rich or poor, cultured or uneducated, young or old, happy or sad, each of us has this yearning within. The child in tears, the teenager in rebellion, the husband and wife with a marriage falling apart, the disillusioned church member, the despondent patient, the lonely retiree—all have this crying need.

Are you willing to listen to them? Should be simple, shouldn't it? But it really isn't. We respond by hogging the spotlight, telling our story, offering our snap judgments.

Jesus always sensed need and responded to it. Love touches off love. He even permitted an irrelevant question to be asked while He was teaching a multitude (Luke 12:13). And in answering the question, Jesus developed another great teaching session by stating, "A man's life consisteth not in the abundance of the things which he possesseth" (Luke 12:15), followed by the illustrating parable of the rich fool (vv. 16-34).

Jesus dealt with the needs of people in a variety of ways. He had no pat answers and used no set formula. People were not treated as robots. They were approached as individuals with each one deserving special personal attention.

GOOD MAN—BAD WOMAN?

A preacher delivered two sermons based on John 3 and John 4. The first, entitled "The Salvation of a Good Man," was about Nicodemus. The second, "The

Salvation of a Bad Woman," was about the woman at the Samaritan well. The point is that goodness or badness, man or woman, makes no difference. Men and women whether good or bad are lost (Romans 3:23).

Jesus was en route from Judea to Galilee. It was dangerous for a Jew to travel through Samaria. There was bad blood between the Jews and this "hybrid" race.

For several reasons Jesus could have bypassed a conversation with the Samaritan woman. *She was a woman,* and a respectable man shouldn't converse publicly with a woman, especially if she was not an acquaintance. In fact, a proper Jewish man of that day would not be seen talking with a woman in public, not even his own wife or mother. Jews had "nothing to do with Samaritans." *She was a sinful woman,* an outcast even among people of questionable morals.

But Jesus talked with the woman. This was why He *"must* needs go through Samaria." He saw her sins. He saw her needs. He didn't talk down to her. There's a big difference in how you listen and how you talk to people. And they know the difference.

The story of Jesus and the woman at the well is the greatest example of personal evangelism to be found in the New Testament. We can learn how from the Master Teacher and Soul Winner.

Jesus sat at Jacob's well. A woman came for water. Weariness fled. Here was one who needed help. Watch His approach.

1. Jesus made contact through a courteous request (v. 7). He neither ignored her nor condemned her, but rather appealed to her sympathy and the better side of her nature.

2. He aroused her curiosity in order to turn her attention to spiritual things. Why would He, a Jew, speak to her? What did He mean by living water? Was He greater than Jacob?

3. He took her aroused sense of need and faced it with an appeal to her conscience. He brought her from the need of securing natural water, a materialistic need, to the need of getting the water of life to satisfy her spiritual need.

4. He continued to deal patiently with her when she tried to cloud the issue with a theological controversy. Her questions were an attempt to change the subject. The Master used the questions to bring her back to the basic issue.

5. He revealed himself to her. She needed to know about this life-giving water and who it was that offered it.

Arguments Generate a Lot of Heat But Create Very Little Light

When Jesus said, "Give me a drink," He was saying, "We have something in common. We are both at the well, and we are both thirsty." Instead of granting His simple request, the woman began arguing with Him. Jesus was more concerned with winning her than winning an argument. The Master Fisherman put out some bait: "If you only knew what a wonderful gift God has for you, and who I am, you would ask Me for some *living* water" (v. 10, *The Living Bible Paraphrased*).

Jesus' request for a drink had disarmed the woman. The request had touched on a common interest—thirst. The approach was neither artificial nor theatrical. Jesus was genuinely thirsty and tired, and He was sincere.

The figure of water is used throughout the conversation. The woman knew from experience that not only Jacob's well but all the world's wells failed to satisfy. Water from earthly wells satisfies for the time, but thirst comes back. Write it on every man-made well of earth: "Thirst again!" The well of pleasure? "Thirst again!" The well of power? "Thirst again!" The well of fame? "Thirst again!" The well of wealth? "Thirst again!"

DRINKING FROM EMPTY CUPS

Flatus and Feliciana are two of the characters in William Law's book *A Serious Call to a Devout and Holy Life*. Both of them spend their days drinking from empty cups.

Flatus jumps from one cup to another. First, he seeks to satisfy himself with fine clothes, then the dice game, social events, drinking. When these fail to satisfy he turns to the big game hunt, followed by getting into the dog breeding business. From that he goes to building projects, then horses, followed by travel. The next empty cup is developing appreciation for the fine arts, and then to top it off, he takes up jogging.

Feliciana tries to slake her thirst with the cup of fine clothes, the theater, the opera, the mad rush of social events, parties, bridge, the gaming table until the early morning hours.

Happiness is momentary, but always there follows tormenting emptiness. But not so the "well of water springing up into everlasting life." The water that finds its source in God finds its ultimate level in God

and always satisfies completely. Because desires are
satisfied, thirst is slaked. One may drink and be
reborn. Little wonder that the woman cried, "Give
me this water."

THE ISSUE

Salvation is essentially a dealing with sin. To find
Christ and His salvation, we must face up to sin as
a personal issue. Do we seek peace of heart and
mind? First, we must acknowledge sin, repent and
accept pardon. Do we seek a new horizon, a sense of
reality? We must renounce all that smacks of evil.
We can't drink from the fountains of God and the
broken cisterns of the world.

Obviously, the woman was hedging, fencing. As a
prostitute she felt uneasy in the presence of the Holy
One. Jesus brought her face-to-face with her sin in
the one little command, "Go and get your husband."
Badly shaken, she burst out, "I have no husband."
In a moment her whole life spread out before her.

Still hedging, the woman tried a new tack. As
Jesus probed her conscience, she set up a smoke
screen to cancel out the convicting word. She deftly
changed the subject to more comfortable ground. She
began to talk about the place where she worshiped.

Our comments are so similar: "My family have been
members of this church for generations."

But Jesus isn't much interested in how many generations the family name has been on the church roll.
He points out instead that it isn't *where* you worship
but *how* that counts.

Poor woman! She didn't know to whom she was
talking. For all her sin, she wanted to be religiously
correct. While answering her questions, Jesus held
her to the essentials. First, there was the truth about

God, then the truth about worship, and finally the truth about himself. The extent of this revelation, packed into so few words, is amazing, especially considering that it was given, not to a brilliant and religious intellectual such as Nicodemus but to a sinful Samaritan woman. That was enough truth to occupy her mind for the rest of her life and then into eternity. Is it any wonder that her testimony brought many Samaritans to Christ's salvation (vv. 39,41)?

HEALING BY REMOTE CONTROL

The second miracle John chooses to record—he presents seven—is the healing of the nobleman's son. The father, an officer in Herod's court, lived at Capernaum. His boy became very sick. Doctors could give no hope and the end was near. Learning that Jesus was back at Cana, the father rushed across the 28 miles. Finding Jesus, the man came right to the point. He "besought him that he would come . . . and heal his son."

There was a lot of shallow believing in Galilee just as there was in Jerusalem and as there is today. But the royal court officer stood in contrast to the crowd in Galilee just as Nicodemus did in Jerusalem.

Jesus tested the father in two ways. First, He made the man's request the occasion for rebuke: "Except ye see signs and wonders, ye will not believe." Then He refused to go to Capernaum, but rather compelled the man to accept a statement for which he could have no immediate evidence.

"And the man believed." He left Capernaum in anxiety but returned resting in faith. What made the man go to Cana? Was it not that he knew of the miracle at the marriage feast? One miracle by Jesus inspires faith to believe for another. Faith feeds on faith and develops faith. It anchors to God's Word. Unbelief feeds on doubt and increases unbelief. Are you feeding on faith or unbelief?

CLASSIFIED AD

FOR SALE: OLD CRUTCHES in fair condition. Will sell cheap. See at 5:1-16 John Street.

Crutches were no longer needed when Jesus performed a third miracle—the healing of a man imprisoned by paralysis for 38 years.

The Bible says, "Jesus went up to Jerusalem." Now when a churchman goes to the city where his church headquarters are, he drops in at the headquarters office. But Jesus, while going up to Jerusalem, went down to the pool of Bethesda by the sheep market. Why? Because there was human need. What about us? Where do we peg our attention?

Bethesda was a mineral spring. Hundreds gathered by its troubled waters for healing. But the cripple who'd hoped for help for 38 years was without anyone to put him into the pool. He was helpless, hopeless, and abandoned—so near and yet so far. He was sinful. His sinfulness may have caused his trouble for Jesus reminded him to sin no more lest a worse thing should come upon him.

How many are caught like this paralytic—"I have no man." Will you be the one to bring that person to the Master?

SWIMMING LESSONS?

"Would you like to get well?" What a strange question to ask an imprisoned paralytic. But not everyone desires help. Some coddle and nurse their troubles.

32

As Billy Sunday put it, "Instead of drowning their troubles, they take them out and give them swimming lessons."

"Do you want to be changed?" Do you want to live victoriously over sin and self? It calls for a cross, self-denial, rigid discipline. Do you really want to be made whole?

THE BEGINNING OF THE END

This is the miracle which cost Jesus His life. The events of that Sabbath day near the sheep market brought the undying animosity of the religious leaders of Israel. And they never ceased in their efforts to kill Him until He was nailed to the cross.

While Jesus was healing the helpless cripple, the Pharisees, looking on, rankled with envy and criticism. Their feelings were clothed in religious garb—devotion to the Sabbath. How inconsistent and heartless religion—not Christianity—can be.

To the Pharisees tradition was more important than people. To see their Sabbath rules and regulations observed was more important than to see a cripple walk. We need to be careful lest we become enmeshed in that Christless web. Is our church more important than Christ, the Lord of the Church? Our denominational connections than being a Christian?

WITNESS STEP FORWARD

Throughout the Gospel of John the claims of Christ confront us, claims which can't be ignored. You can sense the mounting tension in the Book, the development of conflict between truth and error, light and darkness, belief and unbelief. Even this early (5:16, 18) His enemies were determined to kill Christ.

33

Men today try to "kill" Christ. Some may do it by claiming a God-is-dead theology. But more dangerous is the proposition that Jesus was a good man, a great teacher—but only that. He was more. He was divine!

To that end Christ calls up His witnesses. The *first* witness is John the Baptist (5:33). He was accepted by the people as a prophet from God. His testimony of Jesus was clear enough for all to believe.

The *second* witness was Christ's works (5:36). The miracle just performed was public knowledge in Jerusalem.

The *third* witness was the Father himself (5:37), but the enemies of Christ were so out of touch with God they were unable to receive His testimony.

The *fourth* witness was the Bible (5:39).

Never forget it—you and I do not receive eternal life by merely knowing the facts of the Bible. We've got to accept the Person of whom the Bible testifies.

Bread That Satisfies

CHAPTER 4/Read John 6

John selects seven miracles, otherwise called signs, to show how Jesus proved His deity.

The Gospel of John also records seven declarations that Jesus made about His deity. Jesus declared himself to be the eternal "I Am" seven times:

1. I am the bread of life (6:35).
2. I am the light of the world (9:5).
3. I am the door (10:9).
4. I am the good shepherd (10:14).
5. I am the resurrection, and the life (11:25).
6. I am the way, the truth, and the life (14:6).
7. I am the vine (15:1).

These seven declarations were supported by seven miracles or signs:

1. Jesus turned the water into wine (2:1-11).
2. He healed the nobleman's son (4:46-54).
3. He healed the paralytic at Bethesda (5:1-9).
4. He fed the 5,000 (6:1-14).
5. He walked on the water (6:15-21).
6. He healed a man blind from birth (9:1-11).
7. He raised Lazarus from the dead (11:38-44).

Two of Jesus' miracles are recorded in the 6th chapter of John. The first is the feeding of the 5,000 and the other is an eyewitness account of Jesus walking on the water.

The prophetic utterance, "Knowledge shall be increased" (Daniel 12:4), is finding fulfillment in the 20th century as in no other. Science as we know it today is largely a product of this century. Ninety percent of all the scientists who have ever lived in the history of the world are alive today. Over 50 percent of all the money spent by the United States on scientific research since the founding of the country was spent during the last 10 years.

People in the first decade of this century were living in the days of the first telephones perfected for general use, the first express trains, the first uses of electricity, the first internal combustion engine.

Then came the automobile with the ribbons of concrete from coast to coast making Americans mobile. Radio and television have changed our patterns of living. The latest news, music, drama are brought right into our homes.

The jet liner has become commonplace. Leave London, enjoy an early breakfast, arrive in New York for breakfast, and you can be in Los Angeles for a late breakfast.

Radar enables us to see in the dark, and electric eyes open doors at our approach. Atomic energy, laser beams, and on and on.

The advances in medical science are phenomenal. For example, crippling polio, a scourge during my youth, has been conquered.

Scientists and researchers produce a multitude of products from synthetics. Now we have synthetic eggs and sausage for dieters which are advertised to taste like the real thing.

But none, no one, can do what Jesus can do. The

most brilliant of men can never feed 5,000 with five barley loaves and two small fishes. That requires a miracle!

The feeding of the 5,000 is the one miracle performed by Jesus which is recorded in all four of the Gospels.

You Can't Run From Need

After the disciples had returned from a brief evangelistic tour, Jesus took them into the wilderness for a time of privacy and rest. But there was no rest for the weary. Their movements were noted and the people flocked to them. Actually, the crowd numbered more than 5,000, for the number referred only to the adult men and did not include the women and children.

Christ was immediately concerned for the famished thousands. Jesus has concern for our physical needs. "Spirituality" which ignores the importance of physical need is not spirituality. When Elijah suffered a nervous breakdown, God didn't condemn him for wanting to give up, to die. The Lord gave him a meal, sleep and a 40-day vacation. Jesus performed one of His mightiest miracles to meet material needs. We should practice deeds of common kindness. It can be the finest means of introducing Christ to those with spiritual needs.

Jesus surprised Philip with the question, "Where can we buy bread to feed all these people?" Philip did his best to figure this out, but the result was disappointing.

A quick mind to calculate ways and means was Philip's strong point. But we must rid ourselves of the weakness of our strong points when dealing with God. When we are strong in ourselves we are spiritually weak. Paul said, "When I am weak then am I strong." Ability to meet the need comes from God and His resources.

Andrew, Philip's friend, scouted around looking for food, but he didn't do much better than Philip. He found a boy who had "five barley loaves and two small fishes." Andrew saw no possibilities in the boy and his picnic lunch: "But what are they among so many?"

Little Can Be Much

Both Philip and Andrew made the mistake of leaving Jesus out of their calculations. But how great the grace of God. He still allowed them to have a part in the miracle. "Make the men sit down . . . and when he had given thanks, he distributed to the disciples, and the disciples to them that were set down" (John 7:10,11).

And Jesus made room for a small boy to have a part in it, too. "There is a lad here." The potential was always there. There was something about Jesus as He reached toward the boy, that the lad without hesitation gave Him all he had.

A few loaves and fishes and thousands of people to feed—a task humanly impossible. The disciples' resources and the task before them were totally disproportionate. But "little is much when God is in it."

To feel the great need of the world is to feel the meagerness of our own assets. But give what you have—your little faith, your partial understanding of His will, the poverty of your nature, the inadequacy of your efforts. The Lord wants what we have. He'll do the rest. He can multiply in a moment to meet the need.

What About the Leftovers

A church leader said, "When I once lose confidence in a man, I never gain it back again."

It's a good thing he's not God. We'd all be lost.

Jesus said, "Gather up the fragments." Jesus always has an interest in leftovers. Fragments of every kind—of our time, of our lives, of our strength.

And that's why Jesus wanted the leftovers picked up—"that nothing be lost." The word is the same as that used of the lost sheep, the lost coin, and the lost son. He is not willing that any should perish. Jesus takes the sin-shattered fragments of human nature and produces saints.

ARE MIRACLES FOR REAL?

God feeds the multitudes all the time by gathering the elements from the air and water, and in the proper proportions. He compounds them in the plants over the growing season of the grain. Farmers harvest their crops, mill their grain, and make bread which sustains life. This is all God's provision.

But Christ's feeding the 5,000 was a rush order which met the emergency of the occasion. This miracle was one of the most dramatic and impressive of all Christ's miracles. It was a miracle of pure creation.

Any attempt to explain away this miracle is to defeat the purpose of God. To describe it in such a way as to make it an event in which natural causes worked themselves out is to oppose the testimony of God's Word.

The miracles of Jesus were for the purpose of instilling belief and life. They are no less effective in their testimony today as the Bible is read. When we learn what Jesus *did*, we are able to accept in faith what He can *do* today.

When we come face-to-face with Christ, we find that we must accept Him as He is presented, miracles and all. The virgin birth of Jesus, His sinless life, His physical resurrection, and His ascension—all miracles —are essential to Christian faith.

The Bible stakes its validity and authority on the miraculous inspiration given to its authors and on the numerous miracles it records. If we reject the miracles, we must reject both Christ and the Bible. Christ, His Word, and His miracles stand or fall together.

The success of the gospel is associated in the Bible with Christ's possession of the power to work miracles. His miracles were the deed of which the gospel was the word.

Miracles are the glory of the Christian faith. They are at the heart of God's relationship to men. They show that God has keen interest in us. He did not create the world and then leave it to operate itself. He still upholds "all things by the word of his power" (Hebrews 1:3).

The feeding of the 5,000 precipitated a stampede to crown Jesus an earthly king. He recognized that their desires were only for material gain—to sweep the Romans out. Jesus saw at once that this was a temptation to evade the cross, to become a king of an earthly kingdom rather than king of a heavenly one. He fled the temptation and went to spend time alone in prayer on a mountain.

WALKING ON WATER

The fifth miraculous event related by John takes place on a stormy sea. The wind was high, and the waves were rough. The disciples were frightened and in very real danger. They struggled till midnight, but, despite being experienced sailors, their cause was about lost.

But the Great Shepherd had concern for His sheep. He is equal to every crisis. Although He had no boat,

He came to them walking on the water. That was a miracle!

It seems to me that there's another miracle connected with this event. The Bible says, "Then they willingly received him into the ship: and immediately the ship was at the land" (v. 21). The disciples had struggled for hours, but when Jesus came aboard they were *immediately* at land. They had been stopped by the storm. Now they arrived instantly.

SLAVES TO THEIR STOMACHS

When the people found Jesus, they asked Him when He had crossed the lake. Instead of answering their question, Jesus put His finger on their selfish motivation. They were not interested in the manifestation of divine power. Their interest was in filling their stomachs again. And this is common among us today—to get all of the material things you can and forget about spiritual matters until some time in the future.

Altogether too many of us are concerned with only the temporal. *Work to make a little money first and then work to make a little money last.*

SEEKERS FOR THE SENSATIONAL

The crowds asked, "What shall we do, that we might work the works of God?" (v. 28). When Jesus informed them all that was needed was to believe on Him, the Christ sent from God the Father (v. 29), they rejected the simplicity of it all. Instead of believing, they asked for a sign that would prove Jesus was the Messiah (vv. 30,31).

In spite of the sign of the loaves and fishes, the Jews still did not see or believe. Sin and prejudice had blinded their eyes. Many today run from one place to another seeking the sensational as the crowd of that day did.

41

You Can't Bake Heaven's Bread
Out of Earth's Dough

Sunday school picnics are fun. Often they are fun at the expense of the pastor or the superintendent. And that's okay.

A preacher was put on the spot at such an event. He was given flour, buttermilk, salt, soda, etc., and told to mix up some biscuits. Well, the culinary arts were not his thing, and he ended up with a gooey mess.

A lot of people are doing the same thing as they try to "make bread" without God. They end up with a mess in their lives. God alone has the recipe, and He alone can provide the ingredients. You can't bake heaven's bread out of earth's dough.

The Claim of Jesus

Jesus said:

I am the bread of life (no Christ-substitutes).

I am the *bread* of life (no bread-substitutes).

I am the bread of *life* (no life-substitutes).

"The people asked, and he . . . satisfied them with the bread of heaven" (Psalm 105:40). That was the manna of the Old Testament. But now we have the true Bread, who is Christ. He is the Loaf broken for us at Calvary, and there is a piece for everyone. He is the only satisfying loaf. But it is ever true that, just as bread will do a starving man no good unless he eats it, so Jesus can't save the sinner who refuses Him.

We can try other breads, but they do not satisfy. In fact, they leave one miserably unsatisfied.

The bread of *wickedness* (Proverbs 4:17) leads to eternal darkness.

The bread of *deceit* (Proverbs 20:17) is "sweet to

a man; but afterward [the] mouth is filled with gravel."

The bread of *idleness* (Proverbs 31:27) brings no praise.

The bread of *mourners* (Hosea 9:4) is reserved for the unfaithful.

The bread of *sorrows* (Psalm 127:2) is tragic food.

The Bread of Life alone can satisfy.

A Turning Point

The masterly discourse on the bread of life marked a turning point in Christ's ministry. Some who had followed Him now "went back, and walked no more with him" (v. 66). They were exposed by the searching judgment of Jesus, "There are some of you that believe not" (v. 64).

His searching question to the twelve, "Will ye also go away?" (v. 67), brought Peter's ringing declaration, "Lord, to whom shall we go? thou hast the words of eternal life. And we believe and are sure that thou art that Christ, the Son of the living God" (vv. 68,69). Peter voiced the sentiment of all true believers.

To whom can we go? Christ is the answer, the only answer. He alone has "the words of eternal life."

He was the Light, yet He hung in darkness on the Cross.

He was the Life, yet He poured out His soul unto death.

He was the Son of God, yet He died a criminal's death.

He was the Lion of the Tribe of Judah, yet He was led as a lamb to the slaughter.

He was the fountain of Life, yet upon the cross He cried, "I thirst."

To Thirst No More

After the TV tube goes dead, *then* what? Turn on the stereo. After the record is played, *then* what? Go to a movie. After the popcorn is finished and the movie is over, *then* what? Jump in the car, get a pizza, *then* what?

This is the meaninglessness of thousands, tightly squeezed into a society of clanging gadgets and fantasyland material things. People try to fill an empty, bored life with things and activities. There is never enough to satisfy the gnawing ache of boredom.

Jesus said, "If any man thirst, let him come unto me, and drink" (7:37) and, "I am the bread of life: he that cometh to me shall never hunger; and he that believth on me shall never thirst" (6:35). *Never* hunger. *Never* thirst. There is complete satisfaction in Jesus. Drink at the well of everlasting life, and life for you will be full.

ANYONE THIRSTY?

The 7th chapter of John records the supreme claim of Jesus and gives the climax of His teaching relative to the life which would result from faith in Him. He literally "cried . . . come unto me, and drink." But before we consider that, let us provide the setting.

The Lord announced His supreme claim during the Feast of Tabernacles held annually in Jerusalem.

The three main festivals of the Jewish religious calendar were Passover, Pentecost, and Tabernacles. Someone said that we may think of them as national religious conventions. Passover was the spring convention; Pentecost was the summer convention; and Tabernacles was the fall convention. Every Israelite male was required to attend all three of these great religious festivals (Exodus 23:14-17).

The Feast of Tabernacles was celebrated as a memorial of the 40 years spent in the wilderness when God fed the Israelites manna and led them with the pillar of cloud and fire. During the seven days of the feast the Jews lived in booths or huts of green branches set up in the streets and even on the flat roofs of the houses. By this they acknowledged their continuing dependence on God even though they now lived in towns and cities.

The feast was a time of rejoicing over the harvest. All the grain, oil, and wine had been harvested. The agricultural year had come to a close. Joy and thanksgiving prevailed. Every Israelite was in holiday attire, with a palm branch in his hand. The temple was brilliantly lighted with great lampstands at night. These lights may well have occasioned Jesus' declaration, "I am the light of the world" (John 8:12).

Jesus did not go to the feast with a party of pilgrims from Galilee but went simply and quietly. En route He ministered to the needs of people, healing lepers, radiating love and comfort, and teaching the gospel. He purposed to arrive at about the middle of the week. Upon arrival He appeared in the temple and with boldness and authority began to teach concerning His mission and the Jews' attitude toward it (7:14-36).

One of the most striking features of the festival was the ceremonial of water libation. Every morning of the feast, while the morning sacrifice was being prepared, a joyous procession with music and headed by a priest bearing a small golden pitcher, made its way from the temple to the Pool of Siloam. The priest filled the pitcher with water and carried it in the procession back to the temple. There, amid loud trumpet blasts, it was poured into a silver basin on the altar.

This high point of the festival was an extremely joyful occasion. It became a proverb: "He that hath not seen . . . the joy of the drawing [and the pouring] of the water hath not seen joy in his life." The spiritually minded saw it as a fulfillment of Isaiah 12:3, "Therefore with joy shall ye draw water out of the wells of salvation."

As is so often the case with regard to spiritual matters, the Feast of Tabernacles had degenerated into mere ritualism by the time that Jesus walked here on earth. As Jesus took in the scene of empty pomp and ceremony, it is no wonder that He could no longer contain himself. Jesus jumped to His feet and cried in impassioned tones, "If any man thirst, let him come unto me, and drink. He that believeth on me, as the Scripture hath said, out of his belly shall flow rivers of living water. (But this spake he of the Spirit, which they that believe on him should receive: for the Holy Ghost was not yet given; because that Jesus was not yet glorified)" (John 7:37-39).

In conversion we receive in our hearts a well of living water to satisfy our thirsty souls. When we are filled with the Holy Spirit, rivers will flow out to water other people's barren souls. The Spirit-filled life is the outflowing life.

WHEN DO WE RECEIVE THE BAPTISM?

The question of whether or not we receive the fullness of the Spirit is quite controversial in many circles. Some believe that a person receives the fullness of the Spirit when he is baptized into the Body of Christ (1 Corinthians 12:13). Others believe that the fullness of the Spirit accompanies sacramental baptism. The claim is then that the experience is "actualized" or "released" when he is baptized in the Spirit.

What does the Bible have to say about the matter? Both John the Baptist and Jesus used the term baptism to describe the infilling of the Spirit (John 1:33; Acts 1:5).

Those who were baptized in the Holy Spirit on the Day of Pentecost were already born again (John 1:12, 13). Their names were already inscribed in heaven (Luke 10:20). Jesus had declared them spiritually clean (John 13:10,11). They had the Spirit with them, but not in them (John 14:16-18). The sinner knows the Spirit in conviction (John 16:8-11); the believer knows Him in regeneration (John 3:5-7), but those who have been baptized in the Spirit know Him in fullness.

HOW DO WE RECEIVE THE BAPTISM?

To be filled with the Holy Spirit means a command is to be obeyed, a promise is to be claimed, and a gift is to be received. The experience is a gift to be received, not a reward to achieve.

While the Bible has much to say about the baptism

in the Holy Spirit, it has little to say as to how we may receive the experience. We gain most of our instruction by observing what the disciples were told to do.

The disciples were told to tarry, which literally means to "sit down" and to remain there for a purpose. They "all continued with one accord in prayer and supplication." God meets those who hunger and thirst after Him (Matthew 5:6; Luke 1:53). The seeker is to ask with intense desire, and continually praise and bless God (Luke 24:53; Psalm 100:4). The work of baptizing believers in the Spirit is God's work. The Bible does not emphasize how we should receive, but how God will give. "He will give . . . He will send . . . He will pour out . . . He will baptize."

Peter exhorted his questioners to "repent" (Acts 2:38). Known sin must be confessed. God gives the Holy Spirit "to them that obey him" (Acts 5:32). Associated with repentance is faith. Faith is the condition on which God bestows all His gifts—salvation, sanctification, healing, the gifts of the Spirit. In like manner, the baptism of the Spirit is received by faith (John 7:39).

Finally, the seeker after the things of God is urged to "take." The last chapter of Revelation states, "And whosoever will, let him take the water of life freely" (22:17). This word "take" is the same word that is translated "receive" in the passages relating to receiving the Spirit.

JESUS BRINGS DIVISION

The Gospel of John gives testimony not only to the deity of Christ and the promise of new life to His followers, but also of the development of both faith and unbelief.

Evidently the consensus of the leaders in John 7 was entirely against Jesus, with only a few individuals willing to believe. This is a meaningful commentary about conditions today. The evidence of God's presence and blessing in any learning experience is in the changed lives encountered.

JOYOUSLY POSITIVE

Christianity is not a long list of don'ts—of prohibitions and negatives. Christianity is joyously positive.

Listen to a parent. "John is such a good boy. He doesn't pop pills. He doesn't drink. He doesn't smoke. He doesn't run around all night." Thank God for that! And we would to God that all young men were like that. But goodness alone will never get us through the pearly gates.

We travel down the road of evasion, of rationalization, of excuse, of alibi, of deceit. We try to fool ourselves. But really, do you want to be plastered with a coat of whitewash? The halo has tumbled off most people.

The Bible leaves no room to question that God hates sin. Nothing too strong can be said about sin. Sin is real, unclean, harmful, destructive, and brings eternal death.

But God loves the sinner. The wonder of the gospel is that sin can be forgiven, cleansed, and forgotten by God!

WHEN JESUS WROTE IN THE SAND

There was this sinful woman, caught in the very act of adultery. Self-righteous religionists wanted her stoned. They had no love for God or zeal for righteousness. They schemed to trap Jesus on the horns of a dilemma.

The woman caught in adultery was an unwilling actress. She had broken the 7th commandment. You can't minimize her sin. As she, a lone figure, stood before her accusers, we might ask, "Where is her partner in sin?" They practiced the same double standard that we practice today. Rather sickening, isn't it, to listen to men in high position and low pour out accusations when their own closet is filled with worse skeletons.

The Scribes and Pharisees had no compassion for the woman, no tears for her sinfulness. They exploited her for their shameful purpose just like the man who seduced her. They didn't look on her as a person. They looked upon her as a thing, a tool to be used and discarded.

The attitude of Jesus was absolutely amazing. He could have judged her. He was without sin. He alone could read her motives and know her heart. He saw that what she needed was not a judge, but a friend.

The procedure by which Jesus dealt with the situation is famous and has become a classic in wisdom. He quietly stooped down, and with His finger wrote in the sand. Ever wonder what He wrote?

The men could have handled her judgment without approaching Jesus. Listen to His words, "He that is without sin . . . let him cast the first stone."

"And they . . . being convicted by their own conscience went out one by one . . . and Jesus was left alone, and the woman." And then the words, "Neither do I condemn thee: go, and sin no more." Jesus didn't condone sin, but He forgave the sinner.

LIGHT FOR THE BLIND

Following the festival in Jerusalem Jesus declared, "I am the light of the world." That claim needed proof. John furnishes it. Jesus became the giver of sight to a blind man. The Gospels reveal that Jesus gave sight to three specific blind men. This was the only one of the three who was *born* blind.

You Can't Deny the Facts

Aroused almost to fury by the healing on the Sabbath day of the man born blind, the Pharisees tried to convince the public, and maybe themselves, that it was a miserable trick performed by a miserable sinner (v. 24).

The Pharisees, the wise and proud and self-exalted Pharisees, were trying to browbeat a simple fellow who had received his sight into saying it was not so. How could he possibly say that? He'd been blind since birth, and everyone knew it. Ridiculous? Yes, and yet the Pharisees tried it. Unable to corner his parents into denying the healing, they applied the pressure on the man himself.

It didn't work. The fellow wouldn't bend. He had courage and more wisdom than the self-righteous religionists. He answered that he didn't know whether Jesus was a sinner or not, but he did know that he couldn't see until Jesus came along. Let them explain that, if they could!

Picture the plight of the Pharisees. Before them was the *fact* of the miracle; the Pharisees tried to deny it with a *theory*. They tried to deny the miracles of our Lord, but the nameless man answers, "Once I was blind, but now I see." How could they account for that? That's the question—how?

And then the Pharisees claimed they were disciples of Moses, but they did not know Jesus. How then could they claim that Jesus was an imposter. The trap closed on them. In effect the man said that never before in all time had one man given another man back his sight. "If this man were not of God, he could do nothing." The implication is there: that's all you've done for me, nothing.

Whipped and beaten by a man ignorant and untrained in theology, the Pharisees were in a rage. They gave vent to their anger by throwing him out of the synagogue.

Two Kinds of Days

There are two kinds of days in our lives. Some days are uneventful. Only a wife can be interested in what her husband did, whom he saw, what he heard. And she does it because she is interested in him. Because she loves him.

But once in a while we experience a momentous day. It literally turns us around. We're never the same again.

The day this blind man was healed was this kind of a day. For the first time he saw the brightness of the sun, the beauty of the skies and trees, flowers, and grass, and the faces of those about him.

One person made the difference; His name was Jesus. What a difference a day can make when Jesus passes by.

The disciples questioned, "Why was this man born blind? Was it a result of his own sins or those of his parents?" And the Pharisees were critical of the procedures that Jesus followed.

Whereas the disciples looked for the human cause, Jesus looked for the divine purpose. The disciples looked for past explanations; Jesus looked at future possibilities. Speculations on the reason for catastrophe are not nearly as profitable as zeroing in on the possibilities of God's mighty intervention. While others were *talking* about the problems, Jesus was *doing* something about them.

How Safe You Are!

CHAPTER 6/Read John 10

In *Future Shock* Alvin Toffler tells us there will be more changes in the next 20 years than in the past 2,000.

This generation has adopted change as a life-style. Anything that smacks of permanence is viewed with suspicion. After all, if mechanization and medicine can be improved, why not man and morals?

Toffler further states that our preoccupation with change "spawns in its wake all sorts of curious social flora—from psychedelic churches and 'free universities' to science cities in the Arctic and wife-swap clubs in California."

Some things don't change. Sin is the same. God's wrath on sin is the same. Salvation is the same. Christ is the same, yesterday, today and forever.

Chiseled on the tombstone of Karl Marx in Highgate Cemetery, outside London, are these words, "Philosophers have interpreted the world, but the point is to change it."

The doctrine of Marxism has changed the world, but it has not brought happiness. Every effort of man to solve his problems, economically, politically, or socially has ended in utter futility.

Religions have dominated the lives of earth's millions through the centuries. But Christianity alone has met the crying needs of men. Christ alone has the solution, for He alone understands the problem.

But to find that solution in Christ we must do something. We must enter His door of salvation. Many wish to change the way to satisfaction, but the changeless Christ alone can meet the unchanging needs of a changing society.

Jesus used familiar scenes as illustration for His messages so that people would undertand the truth He was teaching. One day He talked about a shepherd and His sheep. He said, "I am the good shepherd" (v. 11) and "I am the door" (vv. 7,9).

WHAT'S A DOOR FOR?

A door is an opening in a wall to allow passage through the wall. If there were no wall, then no door would be needed. The door is significant because the wall separates; it shuts out and shuts in.

What is the value of the door? When is it important? A door is only of value when it is used, when people can go in and out.

Mrs. Winchester, the widow of the manufacturer of the Winchester rifle, was a multimillionaire. She spent a fortune over about three decades building a house of 161 rooms. Scores of doors were false; they opened to solid walls. What a way to spend a fortune!

But eccentric ways are not limited to just a few. Religionists design elaborate doors that open to solid walls. To follow such leaders is to come to the end of the road with no exit, nothing but a dead end. How tragic!

Sin has separated us from God. Our sin has shut us out from the presence of a holy God. His righteousness can't permit our entrance into heaven because of our unrighteousness. But in love He provided a doorway. When He sent His Son to take our place as condemned sinners at Calvary, the door was opened.

Jesus became the doorway into the presence of God. He said, "I am the door." He is not only the *door;* He is the *only* door. There is no other access to God.

THE WOLF CAN'T GET IN

A sheepfold was an enclosure in which several flocks of sheep were gathered for safekeeping during the night under the care of a porter. In the morning the porter opened the door of the sheepfold for each shepherd as he came to call out his own sheep.

Sometimes there was no door. Dr. George Adam Smith was talking with an Arab shepherd, a non-Christian. "Where," said the shepherd, "do the sheep go at night? They go into an open cave that has no door. I am the door. When the light has gone and all the sheep are inside, I lie in that open space, and no sheep ever goes out except across my body, and no wolf comes in unless he crosses my body. I am the door."

Participation in church ritual, observance of the sacraments (baptism and communion), devotion to good works, manifestation of social concern—none of these are doors to heaven. Jesus is *the* door. There is no way to get into the kingdom of God except through Christ. All competitors are designated "thieves and robbers" coming "to steal, and to kill, and to destroy."

DON'T HIRE A HIRELING

Church leaders can be hirelings instead of shepherds (v. 12). The healing of the blind man in chapter 9 of the Gospel had created great excitement. The leaders of organized religion were the self-appointed shepherds of their day, but their behavior was anything but shepherdlike. They were selfish, envious, heartless. They were more interested in the fleece than the flock. Their act of excommunicating the poor blind man for daring to be loyal to the One who had opened his eyes revealed their true character. Tyrannical ecclesiasticism wherever it may be found is unchristian.

Through the centuries men have come in their own name laying claims to spiritual greatness. They have been false prophets, speaking without a divine commission. Such leaders always got a following and always will.

But the Lord's sheep are given a remarkable deafness to the siren voices of false shepherds. "And a stranger will they not follow, but will flee from him; for they know not the voice of strangers" (v. 5).

Oriental shepherds train their sheep to know their voice. Their calls are words yet not words, music yet not music. The sheep understand and know their own shepherd's voice.

An Arab village had been held responsible for an attack upon a Jewish neighborhood, and the village was required by the authorities to pay a heavy fine. They were not able to raise the cash, and so their flocks of sheep and goats were confiscated. One little Arab boy, an orphan, had 12 lambs and from some source was able to raise sufficient funds to redeem them. He brought the money to the officer and was told that he could have 12 lambs, but it would never be possible to separate his own, so he could have any 12 he wished. The boy said, "Sir, let me try to find my own." He went off to the side of the large flock and gave his shepherd's call. There was a stir among the crowded flock, and one after another certain lambs crowded their way out, and a happy boy went his way with 12 lambs following him.

Sick sheep are the ones which fail to recognize and respond to the shepherd's voice. A healthy sheep follows his shepherd.

New York City has a potter's field where over 2,000 men and women are buried, people who died unknown or friendless. Under the direction of a landscape gardener the place has been made into a beautiful garden by city prisoners. There is only one monument in the vast burial ground, and it bears the inscription, "He calleth his own by name."

Your name may not be widely known to earth's millions, but the important thing is that you claim Christ as Lord and Saviour. And He calls you by name. To Him you are more than a Social Security number or a computer digit. Themistocles boasted that he knew the names of the 20,000 citizens of Athens. But the Good Shepherd knows His sheep by name.

Four "I Am's"

Four times Jesus uses the words "I am" in John 10:7-11: "I am the door" twice, (vv. 7,9); "I am come" (v. 10); "I am the good shepherd" (v. 11).

The "I am" of Provision. "I am the door: by me if any man enter in, he shall be saved, and shall go in and out, and find pasture" (v. 9).

The religious leaders had excluded a man (9:34). Jesus included him (9:35-38). Glorious benefits are provided by way of the door, Christ Jesus.

First, *forgiveness* is assured: "He shall be saved." None will ever come to be turned away (6:37).

Second, *freedom* is promised: He "shall go in and out." No restriction of movement here, no binding as those "under the law." The sheep of Christ's flock are not prisoners, but God's free men. It is no longer *must* but *may*. The restraints of the law are exchanged for the constraints of love. *In* for shelter; *out* for service. *In* for worship; *out* for witness. *In* for safety; *out* for satisfaction. *In* for comfort; *out* for companionship.

Third, *food* is provided: He shall "find pasture." David said, "He maketh me to lie down in green pastures." The Lord provides the pasture, we must do the eating. In other words, the province of the shepherd is to get the sheep where the pasture is. Beyond that the responsibility is on the sheep.

How is your spiritual appetite? Are you feeding on God's Word? Do you receive the strength to be gained by prayer? What about your church attendance?

The "I am" of Purpose. "I am come that they might have life" (v. 10). This is in contrast to the thief that comes to steal, kill, and destroy.

Jesus never once used the word *religion,* as far as we have record, but He always used the word *life.* He came to give life and to give it more abundantly. Our Lord is not content that we have just a spark of life. Unfortunately, we are too often satisfied with that, and have lost the abundance He offers.

We are not called to be anemic, listless, lifeless, but to have the life abounding and the life victorious. Many people simply exist. Christ wants them to *live*.

The "I Am" of Purchase. "I am the good shepherd: the good shepherd giveth his life for the sheep" (v. 11).

Hans Neilson was a shepherd in an extremely remote station on a large sheep ranch in the West. Here he was in charge of a large flock of sheep. He lived alone—except for his dog Shep—in a little range shack which was fitted with the necessary comforts for all seasons of the year. The nearest house and human being were miles away.

After two years there came a dreadfully severe winter. The sheep sheds were old, and the shelter for the sheep was poor. New sheds were to be built in the spring. It was hard for poor Hans, but he succeeded in saving all his sheep until the last and most violent blizzard of all. After it was over, help was sent from the ranch headquarters to see how Hans fared. They found his dead body near the sheep sheds, and Shep standing guard by his master. The sheep were all alive and well, and it was evident to the men that Hans had been trying to place additional protection at the broken places in the old sheds when his brave battle ceased, and he was overcome by the intense cold. He might have saved his life by neglecting the sheep, but he had literally given his life for his sheep.

Jesus looked upon us as needy sheep (Matthew 9:36) and made the supreme sacrifice for us. It must be spelled out in the letters of C-A-L-V-A-R-Y. Creatively the Lord made us; redemptively He purchased us by "the blood of the everlasting covenant" (Hebrews 13:20).

Having given His life for us in death, and having given His life to us in resurrection, our Lord would release that life through us to those who have not known its soul-restoring power. Life for the dead! Life from the dead! Life to the dead!

DOES JOHN 10:27-29 TEACH ETERNAL SECURITY?

"My sheep hear my voice, and I know them, and they follow me: and I give unto them eternal life; and they shall never perish, neither shall any man pluck them out of my hand. My Father, which gave them me, is greater than all; and no man is able to pluck them out of my Father's hand."

With regard to this passage, J. Nelson Parr states, "The words *hear, know, follow,* and *give* in the Greek are all in the present continuous tense, and the literal translation of this passage is as follows: 'My sheep are hearing My voice, and I am knowing them, and they are following Me; and I am giving unto them eternal life.'"

Christ's true sheep keep hearing, keep obeying, and keep following Him. As they do so, He keeps on giving them eternal life.

Jesus came to give us life, eternal life. That life is Christ's life, and we keep on having it only as we keep on hearing, obeying, and following. The conditions are to be fulfilled.

In Christ we have safety and security. Human nature is frail, but thousands testify to the abundant grace and power of God to live the Christian life. Our security depends on not grieving away the Holy Spirit within us.

A swiss guide led a party of climbers along a precipitous Alpine trail. They halted by a gaping crevasse where the rock had broken away, leaving a sheer drop. The guide leaped across the narrow chasm, then turned and called to his party to follow. The first man stepped to the edge, looked down into the yawning gap, lost his courage and turned back. Then the guide held up a great, strong hand. "Look," he ordered. "See this hand? This hand has never yet let a man fall. Jump!" With his eyes on that strong man, the climber leaped into space and was pulled to safety.

Jesus, the Good Shepherd, holds up His nail-scarred

hand and says, "See this hand? This hand has never yet let a man fall. Jump! And I will hold you."

We can reject that strong hand of the Lord. The Bible is full of warnings which show that we can throw away our confidence. The Bible says, "The just shall live by faith." Faith is the channel by which life continues to flow. We must maintain living faith. And "faith comes by hearing, and hearing by the word of God" (Romans 10:17).

How tragic that some renounce the gospel and grieve the Spirit in such a way that God will give them over to spiritual blindness and hardness of heart.

A person is backslidden to a degree when he becomes careless in his Christian life. When he chooses to live in sin he is so backslidden that he loses his place in Christ. The Book of Galatians (5:17-21) lists a catalog of sins and declares "that they which do such things shall not inherit the kingdom of God." If we fall into sin, there is hope if we will confess and forsake our sin. "If we confess our sins, he is faithful and just to forgive us our sins, and to cleanse us from all unrighteousness" (1 John 1:9).

Keep three things in focus:

1. *The work of Christ makes us safe.* "Wherefore he is able to save them to the uttermost that come unto God by him, seeing he ever liveth to make intercession for them" (Hebrews 7:25).

2. *The Word of God makes us sure.* "These things have I written unto you that believe on the name of the Son of God; that ye may know that ye have eternal life, and that ye may believe on the name of the Son of God" (1 John 5:13).

3. *The walk of obedience makes us secure.* "And being made perfect, he became the author of eternal salvation unto all them that obey him" (Hebrews 5:9).

A basic distinction between Christianity and other religions is the confrontations of the disabilities of man with the abilities of God. Religion says "You can." Christianity says "God can." Religion is based on self-realization; Christianity is based on Christ-realization.

Was Jesus Too Late?

CHAPTER 7/Read John 11 and 12

The late Peter Marshall, in his sermon entitled *Go Down, Death,* tells a story of a little boy suffering with an incurable illness. Month after month his mother tenderly cared for him. As the days wore on, the boy began to realize that he wouldn't live. One day he said simply but oh so earnestly, "Mother, what's it like to die? Does it hurt?"

His mother fled to the kitchen to tend to something on the stove as scalding tears rained down her cheeks. But she knew the question had to be faced. A moment long dreaded had come. Her knuckles were pressed white against the wall, and her head pounded like a trip hammer. But she knew how to pray. "Lord, tell me how to answer him." And God did right then.

Coming back to the sickroom, she said, "Kenneth, remember when you were tiny you used to play so hard, when night came you were too tired even to undress, and you would tumble into Mother's bed and fall asleep. That wasn't your bed; it wasn't where you belonged.

"In the morning you would wake up and find yourself in your own bed. Your father had come with big strong arms and carried you away. Kenneth, death is just like that. We just wake up some morning and find ourselves in the other room—our own room, where we belong—because the Lord Jesus loves us."

The little fellow never raised a question again. And several weeks later he fell asleep just as his mother had described. That is what death is like for the Christian. And when we wake in the morning everything will be just right.

DEATH DEALT THE KNOCKOUT BLOW

Jesus of Nazareth made the supreme claim, which no other in all history has dared to make: "I am the resurrection, and the life." And He alone has fulfilled that claim. He raised Lazarus from the grave, and He arose himself.

The series of miracles in the Gospel of John all lead to the crowning miracle of the resurrection of Christ. The final sign pointing to this is the raising of Lazarus. The first (the wedding at Cana) and the last (the raising of Lazarus) of the seven miracles recorded in John take place in the atmosphere of the home. Jesus is the perfect family friend. He was welcomed at the wedding in Cana, and He was needed at the house of mourning in Bethany.

The setting is in Bethany, on the southeastern slope of the Mount of Olives, 1½ miles from Jerusalem. Today it is a cluster of crumbling houses, amid which lies a lonely tomb, cut out of limestone rock, that is said to be the tomb of Lazarus.

Three interesting people lived in Bethany—Mary, Martha and Lazarus—two sisters and a brother.

One of the great treasures of life is to have a home into which we can go at any time and find rest and understanding and peace and love. In the home at Bethany Jesus had just such a place. He had no home of His own. He had nowhere to lay His head (Luke

64

9:58). But here were three people who loved Him, and here He could go for rest from the tensions of life.

One of the greatest gifts that any of us can give to another is the gift of understanding and of peace. To have someone to whom we can go at any time, and know he will not misunderstand us, betray our confidences, or laugh at our dreams. To have somewhere to go where the tensions of life are relaxed in an atmosphere of love and peace is deeply appreciated. You and I can make our homes like that. Money doesn't make it so; lavish and costly hospitality is not required. The only cost is an understanding heart.

Lazarus became seriously ill, and the family turned to Jesus for help. They sent word to Jesus at Perea, east of Jordan, where He was ministering. The contents of their message is interesting: "Lord, behold, he whom thou lovest is sick." This indicated the affection and regard which existed between Jesus and the family. They didn't feel it necessary to tell Jesus what to do; they were confident of His help.

The next two days were agonizing ones for Mary and Martha. "Why didn't Jesus come? If He'd been here, Lazarus would still be living."

Why Did God Let It Happen?

A common question in our hearts when we are in distress is "Why did God allow this to happen to me?" Who among us hasn't felt shattered by some great trial or tragedy? In the raising of Lazarus there is a clear-cut teaching about this problem which we face.

Sickness is not necessarily a sign of alienation from God. There are times when God may use this chastening to bring us closer to himself, but sickness is no evidence that God has turned His back on us. Lazarus was sick, and he was the man whom Jesus loved.

We are prone to want immediate answers to our prayers. "When [Jesus] had heard therefore that he was sick, he abode two days still in the same place." Because Jesus loved this family, He delayed His coming for two days. They were to learn later that this delay and the disappointment that followed would result in greater blessings. The very things that make us think that the Lord has forgotten us may be the proofs of His love. They may be delays of love.

Entering the Lions' Den

Jesus remained for a couple of days and then suggested going to Bethany (v. 7). The disciples realized Bethany was less than 2 miles from Jerusalem, and the last time there the Jews had sought to kill Jesus. To them Jerusalem had become a lions' den.

When Jesus said that Lazarus was sleeping (v. 11) they jumped at the chance. "Let's leave well enough alone and stay here." How easy for the most spiritual among us to miss God's will when our eyes are on circumstances. When Jesus spoke His determination to go to Bethany at all costs, it was Thomas the Doubter who said, "Well, if it's got to be, it's got to be. Let's all go, and—since He's going to die—we'll all die along with Him." Thomas, come what may, wouldn't quit. "There was not expectant faith, but loyal despair."

For Jesus, the will of God, not personal safety was the rule of action. He knew that the plan would not miscarry, that the lions could not devour Him till the divine hour struck—and for that He was prepared.

What Do You Do After a Funeral?

The fear of death falls like a haunting shadow

across the path of our lives. But Jesus has forever removed that fear. He proved this at Lazarus' grave and by His own resurrection.

Jesus came to Bethany. Lazarus' body had been corrupting in the grave for four days.

MARTHA'S "LORD IF . . ."

Martha, the activist, went to meet Jesus the moment she heard of His arrival in town. Her faith had been tried in three ways: (1) by Jesus' absence, (2) by Jesus' delay, (3) by bereavement.

"If You had been here" was Martha's greeting. Do we indulge in similar regrets?

"Lord, if You had been here I could have trusted You." His answer: "Blessed are those who, having not seen, yet believe."

"Lord, if you had been here I could have resisted temptation." His answer: "There hath no temptation taken you but such as is common to man: but God is faithful, who will not suffer you to be tempted above that ye are able, but will with the temptation also make a way to escape, that ye may be able to bear it."

"Lord, if You had been here, I wouldn't have had to suffer." His answer: "Lo, I am with you alway."

Martha had faith, but not perfect faith. She believed that the presence of Jesus would have saved Lazarus from death, and she ventures "even now" (v. 22) God would answer Jesus' prayers. But when Jesus said, "Thy brother shall rise again," her faith took a kangaroo's leap to that great future event—the resurrection.

"Present tense faith found refuge in future tense faith." But the greatest defect in Martha's faith was not so much a matter of time. She had to learn that hope was not in an event but in a Person.

It's exceedingly difficult to say just the right word to those who are grief-stricken. But the Lord Jesus knew exactly what to say. J. H. Jowett said, "When the Lord Jesus breaks the silence, He breaks what makes the silence deadly." Jesus said, "Thy brother shall rise again." Simple words, but Martha's grief prevented her getting their true meaning. And then He uttered the majestic name of God, "I am."

"I am the resurrection and the life." To know this is to know Him, and to know Him is to know life. Martha's faith rose, and she answered the "I am" with a thrilling "Thou art."

THE THERAPY OF TEARS

Mary arrived on the scene, and, while she had been weeping over the loss of her brother, when she saw Jesus she burst into uncontrollable sobs and fell at His feet. Whenever we find Mary in the presence of Jesus, she is at His feet. First, we find her sitting at His feet, learning (Luke 10:39). Later she is kneeling at His feet, anointing them in spontaneous worship (John 12:3). Here she is prostrate at His feet, yielded to His will despite her grief. She has the same words of greeting as Martha: "Lord, if you had been here." But the tone is different.

Mary wept, and the Jewish neighbors joined her. Grief brings tears. There is therapy in tears.

"Jesus wept." He was not a cold, calculating reformer, plotting the next strategic move for personal gain. He wept. Here was a communion of tears. Here was a revelation of the compassionate Saviour. How human He was. In the midst of grieving friends, He, too, grieved—not for Lazarus' death but for those who suffered loss.

TRIUMPH IN THE CEMETERY

Five important words were spoken at the grave—"Take ye away the stone." They had placed the stone on the tomb, and Jesus now called on them to remove it to open the tomb.

We must remember that the Lord calls on us for our cooperation before we know fully what He will do.

The miracle happened. "Lazarus, come forth." It was the voice of Deity calling things that are not as though they were.

IN THE MORNING

Catherine Marshall writes in *A Man Called Peter* of her husband's death.

"The scene was etched forever on my mind—Peter lying on the stretcher where two orderlies had put him down for a moment while the ambulance waited outside the front door. Peter had looked up at me and smiled through his pain, his eyes full of tenderness, and I leaned close to him as he said, 'Darling, I'll see you in the morning.'"

That's what Jesus has done for us. He has promised us a morning.

FOOTSTEPS TO CALVARY

The public ministry of the Lord Jesus is brought to a close in John 11 and 12. In chapter 12 we are in the last week before His death; by the beginning of chapter 13, on the eve of it.

Great events always produce a series of consequences. The anointing by Mary (12:3) was a beautiful sequel to the raising of Lazarus. Her act is possibly the highest expression of love to Christ to be found anywhere in the Gospels.

WHAT'S YOUR MOTIVE?

Mary's act of devotion was motivated by overwhelming love. Martha was serving—service is fine, but don't let it cause you to lose communion. Lazarus is reclining in Roman style at the feast. Mary looks at them all. If it were not for Jesus, Lazarus would not be there. It seemed a while before that Jesus had failed to respond in time, but He had delayed in love to provide a greater miracle.

Overwhelmed with love, she felt she must do something unusual. So she went to her room and got "a pound of . . . spikenard, very costly, and anointed the feet of Jesus." Then she stooped over and dried His feet with her long tresses. Utter devotion and humility were expressed in this act of deep love. Mary took something of *her own*. She paid the full price of the spikenard. This was something that belonged to her and was very precious to her. Preciousness, not cost, reflects the worth of our gifts of love to the Lord.

Judas protested Mary's act. Mary's motive was love; the motive of Judas was selfishness. He was greedy and covetous. The Bible says his protest in reality was not motivated by concern for the poor, but because "he was a thief and carried the bag."

Motive is "that which incites action and moves the will." Jesus' presence at the feast brought many Jews there who wanted to see not only Him but also Lazarus, the walking dead man. This brought the chief priests into consultation. Their evil motives caused them to seek to put Lazarus to death (v. 10).

We need to weigh carefully that which feeds our desires and motivates our decisions. Even when what we do may be defended as right, we need to be sure that we are prompted correctly.

Pious words come easily. A youngster one Sunday afternoon came into the house to tell his father that a neighbor wanted to borrow the lawn mower.

The father was shocked. "What? He wants to cut his grass on Sunday? Tell him our mower is broken."

What does a response like that tell a boy about his father's religion?

One Day a Hero, the Next . . .

The day after the big dinner in Bethany, Jesus made His way to Jerusalem. Great crowds converged on Him. Men, women, and children welcomed Him, strewing His way with their clothes, waving palm branches, and shouting, "Hosanna: Blessed is the King of Israel that cometh in the name of the Lord" (v. 13).

How many in that crowd that day were in the huge crowd who within the week were shouting, "Crucify, crucify!" How fickle are the crowds.

"We've Lost!"

As the crowds hailed Jesus with their hosannas, the Pharisees were driven further in their utter frustration. They had been defeated at every turn—at the healing of the cripple at Bethesda, at the discourse of the Bread of Life, at the Feast of Tabernacles, at the incident of the woman taken in adultery, at the discourse after Tabernacles, in the healing of the man born blind, at the discourse on the Good Shepherd, at the Feast of Dedication, at the raising of Lazarus, at the supper in Bethany, and now at the Triumphal Entry. Little wonder that they said to each other, "We've lost. Look—the whole world has gone after him!" (verse 19, *The Living Bible Paraphrased*).

Show Them What They're Looking For

John in his next story tells of certain Greeks who came to Philip saying, "Sir, we would see Jesus." Whatever else prompted the Greeks to come, they wanted above all to "see Jesus." We are making real progress when we want to see Jesus.

71

A young pastor in his first Sundays in the new pulpit had preached a series of masterly oratory, touching on philosophy and the arts, but containing very little gospel.

One Sunday he found a handwritten note on the pulpit. It read, "Sir, we would see Jesus." At first, resentment rose in his heart. But the faithful Holy Spirit dealt with him. He went before God and bared his heart. God met him and touched him.

The next Sunday found a different man in the pulpit. He stood in humility, but with a heart burning with a message from God.

As he stepped to the pulpit the following Sunday, he found another note which read, "Then were the disciples glad when they saw the Lord."

THE MAGNETISM OF JESUS

Verse 32 is the key verse of chapter 12: "And I, if I be lifted up . . . will draw all men unto me."

What an outstanding claim from One who was considered a failure by His generation. His messages and claims fell on deaf ears for the most part. His miracles were attributed to Satan. He was an ex-carpenter, unordained by the religious establishment. He had incurred the enmity of the religious rulers who even then were plotting His death. He lived all his life and delivered all His claims in a small vanquished country. Soon He was to be a dead prophet.

But what a conqueror! He was soon to be lifted up. Through the centuries multiplied millions have been drawn to Him. He satisfies the needs of all who come.

He Took a Towel . . .

CHAPTER 8/Read John 13

The central point of worship for the children of Israel was the tabernacle in the wilderness, later replaced by the temple in Jerusalem.

Two rooms, one smaller and the other larger, made up the inner area which was surrounded by the court of the tabernacle. The smaller room was known as the Holy of Holies. In the Holy of Holies was the ark with its mercy seat and cherubum. Once a year on the Day of Atonement, and on that day only, the high priest entered this most holy place. The larger room was the Holy Place in which was the altar of incense, table of showbread, and golden candlestick. This room was used daily. The two rooms were separated by a heavy veil.

The first 17 chapters of John have been compared to the Old Testament tabernacle. The first 12 chapters record the public ministry of Jesus and compare to the Court of the Tabernacle. Chapters 13-16 are a record of Jesus' private ministry to His disciples and compare to the Holy Place. Chapter 17 brings us a glimpse of the Holy of Holies as the curtain is pulled aside and we with "shoes removed" and solemn wonder hear the Son hold conversation with God the Father.

Usually chapters 13-16 are called the "Upper Room Discourse." Actually only 13 and 14 pertain to the Upper Room where Jesus celebrated the Passover with His disciples and instituted the Lord's Supper.

The discourse, however, continued as Jesus walked with His disciples from the place of the supper toward the Garden of Gethsemane.

LAST MINUTE INSTRUCTIONS

Whenever my wife and I plan to take an extended trip, we make extensive plans, elaborate preparations, and give distinct last-minute instructions to those who will be in charge of our home. These directions will govern the conduct of affairs while we are away.

In a very real sense, Jesus was preparing for a journey—to the cross, the tomb, the ascension—from which He has not yet returned. During these last hours of His earthly life He places special emphasis on what His followers were to do and how they were to conduct themselves as they await His return.

The Lord's final words to His disciples are the richest, most inexhaustible and profound utterances that ever came from His lips in an extended series. Here we have Christ's final teachings on some of the greatest subjects that can occupy our minds. The eight main themes are: God the Father, Christ the Son of God, the Holy Spirit, the Word of God, Christian life and conduct, the life to come, the world in which we live, and Satan and his work.

While the first three Gospels record in great detail Jesus' words to the unbelieving Jews as well as His great discourse on His second coming (none of which is recorded in John) it is His intimate discourses, uttered shortly before His arrest, that are found exclusively in John.

74

The only matters in John 13 through 17 which are found in the other Gospels are the Lord's Supper and Jesus' predictions concerning two coming tragic events —the coming betrayal by Judas and the coming denial by Peter. There is one more event that is found only in John—our Lord washing the disciples' feet.

The record of these few hours of one day in our Lord's life occupies one-fifth of the entire text of the Gospel of John.

ON TOWELS

Towels come in all sizes and shapes. Some are patterned and some are plain. Hand towels, bath towels, beach towels, dish towels—all are for specific purposes. While some towels may be used to decorate a bathroom, for the most part towels are used to serve human need.

What is the main symbol of Christianity? Very possibly most people would answer, "The cross." No disagreement there. A cross, whether atop a building or carved in wood or stone, indicates a religious connection.

But there are other meaningful symbols of Christianity among which is the towel. And the towel is central in the first half of John 13.

A natural introduction to the text is found in verse one: "Having loved His own . . . he loved them unto the end." He "knew that his hour was come." He knew "that the Father had given all things into his hands" (v. 3). He knew "who should betray him" (v. 11). Knowing all, He loved. What follows, then, is an act of love. Love is "an attitude of undiscourageable good will." Love is always serving others.

The disciples were gathered in an upper room for the Passover. The custom was that, on arrival at a friend's house for dinner, a servant would wash the feet of the guests. This was necessary because they wore sandals and walked over dusty roads. A common courtesy, this was a part of the social routine. But Jesus turned it into something else. There was no servant in the Upper Room. None would condescend to the role. Then Jesus in deepest humility took "the form of a servant" (Philippians 2:7).

In a moment the disciples to a man—with the possible exception of Judas who would only act in pretense—wished that he had taken the towel. When Jesus returned to the table, He found a humbled and shame-faced group of men ready to have driven home to their hearts the powerful meaning of the example which had just been set before them.

Jesus "took a towel." The towel speaks of humble, loving service. Love does not stand on ceremony nor wait for others to show their hand first. Love gives itself away through spontaneous acts of service and devotion.

HAVE YOU TAKEN THE TOWEL?

We can take the towel in many ways. In a certain city several groups of Pentecostal Christians met in their respective cells for many years. They were divided in spirit and formed no common front against sin and Satan in their city. A young couple came to serve one group as pastor. God began to move by His Spirit. People from the other groups began to attend.

The Holy Spirit was present in a marked manner in the service one Sunday morning. Early in the service a large, strong man arose and asked the pastor for permission to speak for a few moments. His wish was granted.

That brother "took a towel." With tears raining down his face, he assumed blame for the devisive spirit among fellow believers. He sobbed for forgiveness. The Holy Spirit led him and that blessed Spirit gripped the audience.

A scene of most holy order took place. Brothers embraced brothers. Sisters embraced sisters. Tears flowed freely among all. The service which began at 11 in the morning continued beyond the noon hour and well into the afternoon.

Differences were settled. Hardness of hearts melted away. Bitterness, rancor, envy, jealousy, pride disappeared. All of these "works of the flesh" (Galatians 5:19-21) were swallowed up in the consuming love of Christ.

The sequel to that beautiful scene was that revival broke out. Many were saved. The Holy Spirit was poured out. Splinter groups came together, and a strong church developed.

The amazing thing about it all was that the man who assumed blame was really not at fault. He "took the towel."

WHAT WE LACK MOST

A common complaint is "There is so little love among us." The words are spoken by church people and by those with no interest in the church. Sometimes it is an observation of regret. Really it's a confession of lack. Do we feel that we are not getting our share of love's affection? Do people and places seem cold? The solution is to love more.

When others seek to discover what selfish motives move us—we are to love. When our love is not desired—we are to love. When we are shabbily treated—we are to love. We are to love as the sun shines. Its rays fall freely on all.

Love reflects itself in our attitude toward Christian obligation. Henry Van Dyke wrote a short story

77

he called "Legend of Service." In it three would-be lovers of the Lord were tested by Him. Each was sent on an errand with the same difficult command to fulfill.

The first servant asked, "Why?"

The second asked, "How?"

The third, who most pleased the Master by his loving trust, asked eagerly, "When?"

THE BADGE OF A TRUE WITNESS

A love that works is important. "By this shall all men know that ye are my disciples, if ye have love one to another" (v. 35). The world does not understand theology or dogma, but it understands love and sympathy. A loving act may be more powerful and far-reaching than the most eloquent sermon.

Conversely, division and strife among believers quickly become known to the world and are the ground for their scornful rejection of the truth which Christians profess to believe and which they ask the world to accept. We surely cannot apply the gospel remedy to a strife-torn world while we are engaged in unlovely battles with one another.

The measure of our rightness with God is the measure of our rightness with our brother. The vertical is measured by the horizontal. We can't be right with God who is above and be wrong with the brother who is nearby. There is an axiom that things equal to the same thing are equal to each other. If that be so—and it is—then, wherever two hearts are right with God, those hearts are right with each other.

WANT TO IMPRESS PEOPLE?

A church congregation that builds a beautiful, sky-piercing edifice will impress the city. The community will stand in awe when they hear about a million-dollar budget. They will surely take note of parking lots overflowing with cars. Impressed? Yes. Convinced? Maybe not. The unsaved man looks for people who show the love of Christ.

Our pronouncements may be ever so good, but there tends to be a wide chasm between our pronouncements and our lives. No such chasm existed in the life of Jesus. His words and His works blended into perfect unity.

Love is nothing if it is not personal. Love is nothing if it is not expressed. Love goes out to others. Love is action based on feelings. That's why people need something more than just to be told they are loved. It's important to tell them; but, unless deeds follow words, the words by themselves count for little.

Don't Waste Your Time

C. S. Lewis advised, "Do not waste your time bothering whether you love your neighbor or not. Act as if you did. As soon as you do this you find one of the great secrets. When you are behaving as if you love someone, you will presently come to love him."

People today feel lonely, isolated, alienated, bitter. Even though they attend a church, some feel unloved, unwanted, depersonalized. Personal relationships that grow out of love can meet this need. Love provided the Saviour, God's greatest gift to us. His enabling for us to love is a great gift. We all grow poorer if we fail to love. Selfish, inward thinking impoverishes us, while love—which always moves outward—enriches us. Let's not waste our "time bothering whether or not" we love someone. Let's get on with doing it.

The Proof of Our Love

Against the dark background of the revelation of

the treachery of Judas (vv. 21-27) and the coming defection of Peter who had just spoken great words of loyalty (vv. 36,37), Jesus nails down the need for obedience.

True love to Christ will be shown by our obedience to His commandments. To profess love without obedience is to parade before the world an obvious contradiction, in fact, a denial of our faith. If we are not submissive to God's commandments, we do not truly love Him.

A mother had three children. Each child came in the morning and said, "Mother, I love you." She asked each one of them to do some little task. The first refused and went his way; the second promised to do his task and promptly forgot it; the third gladly promised and did as he was told. Which child really loved the mother? The answer is simple—the third one who did what mother asked. Love leads us in joy to do our Master's will.

The disciples called Jesus "Master [teacher] and Lord" (v. 13). Jesus reversed the order. He was their "Lord and Master [Teacher]" (v. 14). We listen to the teachings of a master. But we are obligated to obey our Lord.

As Jesus proceeded to wash the feet of the disciples, no one said a word, except Peter; he always had something to say. First, he protested, "Thou shalt never wash my feet." When Jesus answered, "Thou hast no part with me," Peter impulsively cried, "Lord, not my feet only, but also my hands and my head" (v. 9). At that point Jesus made an important statement concerning the matter of cleansing. He instructed Peter, "He that is washed needeth not save to wash his feet, but is clean every whit."

In those days, people went daily to the public baths.

Their feet became soiled as they returned to their homes and it was necessary to wash or to rinse them. Jesus used two different words for *wash,* which convey quite different meanings. Jesus actually was saying that a man who has bathed and then walks home along the dusty roads does not need to bathe all over again, because of his dusty feet. He needs only to have his feet washed.

Or let us put it this way. I take a bath in the morning, but my hands become soiled during the day. I wash them before the noon lunch and at other times during the day.

The Christian is one who has been cleansed by faith in the shed blood of the crucified Christ. But he walks in a soiled world. The defilements of sin are everywhere. The disciples who were in the upper room had become soiled with pride and selfish ambition. All of us can become soiled in one way or another. It is an absolute necessity that we shall have a continuous application by faith of the cleansing blood.

As we keep occupied with God's Word, bathing our hearts and minds in it daily, and walking in its light, we are kept from those thoughts, words, and deeds which would mar fellowship with the Lord.

Sins and failures must be brought instantly to the Lord if we are to maintain unbroken fellowship with Him.

The Cure for Heart Trouble

CHAPTER 9/Read John 14

A survey was conducted in Marion, Ohio, by 66 people, most of them young people, with a few adult counselors. In about one hour 662 people were contacted and asked one simple question: "How does a person get to heaven?" The answers were amazing and shocking. These are samples:

3 said, "Be baptized."

4 said, "I don't care."

23 said, "Keep the Ten Commandments."

27 said, "I'm too busy."

28 said, "I'm not interested."

30 said, "I refuse to answer."

58 said, "Be good."

64 gave answers such as "I don't understand, I speak German"; "Be kind to women"; "Beats me"; "Ask Art Linkletter"; "Up the Golden Stairs"; "Nobody knows"; "Silly question"; "Don't want the place."

77 said, "I don't know."

90 said, "By doing good works," such as "being honest, helping people, obeying parents, living a decent life."

Only 23 said, "By receiving Jesus Christ as personal Saviour and Lord."

In John 14 Jesus told His disciples that He was going to prepare a place for them and return for them. Thomas asked Jesus, "How can we know the way?" to which Jesus responded, "I am the way, the truth, and the life."

GLOOM CAN HANG THICK

The atmosphere of the Upper Room was heavy with grief. All that Jesus said about His going away distressed this little group of followers. He had become their very life, and all their hopes were in Him. Judas, the traitor, had gone out to accomplish his nefarious deed.

Human nature can be disillusioning. Not only was there a traitor in the small band of apostles, but even one of those who really believed—the spokesman at that—had been warned by Jesus that he would deny Him before morning. Peter had stoutly declared, "I will lay down my life for thy sake." Soon he was to slump to an act of cowardly denial of the Master.

The gloom seemed thick enough to slice with a knife. They must have been thinking, "One of us is a traitor. And apparently we can't trust even Peter. Who can we trust? Can we trust even ourselves?"

Jesus knew that these events were but the beginning. The disciples were going to see Him denied, abused, unfairly tried, reviled, and crucified. Satan would seemingly triumph in these hours of darkness, and what darkness!

Knowing all things, and how the blow was to fall upon these dear men who had walked and worked so faithfully with Him, Jesus said, "Let not your heart be troubled: ye believe in God, believe also in me." True, Jesus was going away from them; sadly true, they had no stability in themselves. But He was not deserting them. The very purpose of His going was for their sakes, "to prepare a place" for them and to come again for them (vv. 2,3). The ultimate welfare of the disciples was very much in focus. They were looking for a secular kingdom, but He promised them a spiritual and heavenly inheritance.

LIFE'S NOT EASY

Little do you know what lies before you. Situations arise which you can't understand. Your hopes may be dashed to the ground, and your heart may be crushed. When all else fails and all is seemingly swept from under you, never forget the loving concern and care of our Lord is always there.

Have you ever had to readjust your life? Change your opinions? Adjustments must be made by all of us. Some adjustments are easy and enjoyable; others are difficult and heart rending. But Jesus will always be there. He not only makes the promise of peace (v. 27), He bestows it in the midst of our turmoil.

Realizing that human beings are so limited in their natural experience, Jesus spoke the assuring words, "If it were not so, I would have told you so."

Desperate sickness comes—but there is still the Great Physician. Death comes—but there is always the empty tomb in the Garden. Jesus is telling us that we are never without His presence. We need never feel alone, nor afraid. God is still master of the universe, and He is dependable. *Believe in Him!*

Believe in Jesus. He is with us. We are told that Napoleon ran far ahead of his troops during the disastrous retreat of the French from Moscow, making sure of his own safety while his men died in the snow behind him. Not so with Jesus. He walked into the jaws of death before the rest of them died. And He came back! An empty tomb is the witness!

WHEN LIFE IS GONE

The soft tones of the organ are silenced; the flowers are fading; the friends are gone. Then like an awesome shroud the finality of death settles. "Where is my loved one? What is there beyond the grave? What's left for me?"

The desire to know what there is beyond this life is present in the heart of every person. Without respect to fame or fortune, creed or culture, youth or old age, the questions lurk: What's in the future, and what sense of assurance and security can I have for life beyond the grave?

Apart from God, we know no rest of spirit. We are constantly aware of a missing dimension of life. Heartache, sorrow, loneliness, and death are with us. The emptiness of separation from God remains unsatisfied until. . . .

JESUS PROVIDES THE ANSWER

Jesus declared, "I am the way, the truth, and the life" (v. 6). Here the Lord Jesus gave to His disciples that truth which they needed so much, the truth which we need. He is the answer to our questions, the allaying of our anxieties, the solution to our problems.

Christ is the Way without error, the Truth without darkness, the Life without end. Not the road marker, but the Road; not the truth teacher, but the Truth; not the lifegiver, but the Life. Not a way, but the only Way; not one segment of truth, but the Truth; not one way of life, but Life itself. Christ alone is the source of life. It is Christ altogether or Christ not at all.

"No man cometh unto the Father, but by me." There is an old saying that all roads lead to Rome. But there is only one Road to God and that is through Jesus by faith in His shed blood. Without the Way there is no going; without the Truth there is no knowing; without the Life there is no living.

85

The words *truth* and *life* explain in what sense He is the Way. He is the Way to God because He is the Truth about God and the source of Life that can't die.

Have you ever been lost and didn't know where to go? Recently a terrible blizzard raged through several of our northern states. Over 50 perished, several of whom struck out from their stranded cars only to get hopelessly lost and die in the fury of the storm.

Hopelessness gripped the disciples when Jesus announced His impending departure. Up to that point, they had walked with Him. They had seen His miracles—water turned to wine, the remarkable healings, the feeding of the 5,000, walking on the sea, the opening of blind eyes, the raising of Lazarus. Now as He drew near to the cross, that path seemed about to come to a dead end. We can hardly understand all that it meant to the disciples to hear that Jesus was to be the Way forevermore. In Him they—and we—were to fight and win and to reach the glory world to stand in the presence of the Father.

CHEER UP!

"Let not your heart be troubled." That word is for us also. When our times of anxiety come we need to be able to trust and not be afraid. When overwhelmed with responsibility we can find strength and courage in Christ.

The disciples kept insisting on their need for a clearcut description of the destination while Jesus calls their attention to the realities at hand. If He is the Way, must we see the end of the road? If He is the Truth, must we be in possession of all the facts? If He is the Life, why can't we enjoy the adventure on a daily basis?

An old martyr was to be burned at the stake. As the preparations were completed, the martyr turned to his judge and said, "Sir, I would that you would come and place your hand over my heart, and see whose heart beats faster." There is a peace to be found in God that can help us move through life's greatest difficulties with a calm heart.

OUR POWER OF ATTORNEY

My brother has been a missionary for many years. When he left America he gave me a legal instrument to act on his behalf. He gave me a power of attorney which is legal written authority from one person to another to act for him. This power of attorney authorizes me to draw checks on his bank account and to sign any legal documents for him.

Jesus said, "If ye shall ask anything in my name, I will do it" (v. 14). The late P. C. Nelson said that in essence Jesus' statement was so encompassing that it carried the meaning of "If we don't have it in heaven, we will make it for you."

Whatsoever we ask for Jesus' sake and endorse in His name, God's bank will pay. We have a blank check handed to us. The Lord also stated that those who believe will do greater works (v. 12). The earthly ministry of Jesus was limited to a few hundred square miles. For us the field is the world.

THE CURE FOR HEART TROUBLE

Faith in Jesus is the cure for heart trouble. Only if we trust can we be still. If we can shift the responsibility of our life on the the Lord's never-failing care, burdens and tears can be exchanged for carefree, radiant, and unspeakable joy.

Faith in Jesus bring obedience to His Word. The world says that seeing is believing. Jesus says that believing is seeing. Obey His precepts, follow His footsteps and we will enjoy His fellowship.

Faith in Jesus will make our lives the channel through which the Holy Spirit can work.

Just Like Jesus

In His final discourse to the disciples, Jesus again and again reverts to the subject of the Holy Spirit. This repeated promise that He would send the Holy Spirit to them was made against the background of His own experience. His miraculous birth into our human race was the work of the Holy Spirit. The Holy Spirit descended upon Him at His baptism. He was led by the Holy Spirit, He was "full of the Holy Ghost," and went forth "in the power of the Spirit." By the Spirit He cast out demons, and "through the eternal Spirit [He] offered himself without spot to God." And the "Spirit . . . raised up Jesus from the dead."

For a brief time Jesus had been Comforter, Paraclete, Helper to His disciples. Now He was about to leave them. He knew that they would need a divine enabler. His own bodily presence was but a temporary arrangement, but He planned permanent help in the abiding presence of the Holy Spirit, whom He called "another Comforter."

As another Comforter, the Holy Spirit would be invisibly and spiritually everything Jesus had been to His disciples visibly and literally during the three and one-half years of their fellowship with Him.

The Holy Spirit was to be given to the disciples. He is a gift in the form of a Person.

The Holy Spirit Is for You

To receive the Holy Spirit is not the luxury of a few; it is a necessity for all. He comes as a personal

Comforter (v. 16) for times when we need comfort and strength, as a personal Companion (v. 16) in times of joy, and a personal Counselor (v. 26) to teach us.

An Englishman and an American were viewing Niagara Falls. Taking the Englishman to the foot of the falls, the American said, "Sir, there is the greatest unused power in the whole world."

"No, no, my friend," replied the Englishman, you're wrong. The greatest unused power in the world is the Holy Spirit of the Living God."

GENUINE PEACE

Americans know more about outer space than about inner peace. Jesus promised peace to His followers (v. 27).

Peace wears many and varied costumes. Peace may be real or illusory. Some have the peace of ignorance, simply because they are uninformed. Others have pretended peace. Like an ostrich with his head in the sand, they live in an unreal world, refusing to face reality. Then there is the peace of fatalism. What will be, will be, rules their life. Apathy and helplessness follow. Still another group seeks the peace of escape. They drown their troubles in liquor, dope, debauchery, a mad whirl of pleasure, or even in becoming a slave to work. Champagne at night with real pain in the morning.

But the only real peace is God's peace. To have God's peace is to accept things as they are, not with despairing fatalism but in trusting confidence. In ourselves we have two choices, anxiety or false security. We are either distracted by trouble or we seek refuge in unreality. False peace places us at the mercy of the circumstances. The peace of God enables us to maintain equilibrium. It's not "*under* the circumstances" but "in spite of the circumstances."

LET THE SUNSHINE IN

A young Christian was riding through a severe storm with an older woman whose life was so very exemplary—completely devoted to God. The new Christian had grown up with a fear of thunder and lightning and expressed her trepidation that day as the storm broke forth from a black, threatening sky.

"I have never forgotten her reply," said the young woman. " 'But the Lord is in the storm!' and indeed she never felt nor showed any anxiety. In the years that followed God gave me complete deliverance from fear also. And how grateful I am for such genuine peace in the midst of the storm! As a mother it became imperative that I avoid passing on any fear of the storm to my children. The quiet declaration of that Christian woman never left me, and eventually I knew the peace that truly passes all understanding during the more severe storms of the human spirit, and my children never learned to fear the storm from their mother."

Jesus knows when you feel closed in with despair and disappointment. He sees you when you are frightened and alone. He is concerned about the problem you face. He wants to open the doors closed by fear and throw open the windows which have been barred by disappointment. The abiding peace of Christ can be yours. He will give you assurance through each day's responsibility with their allotments of joys, trials, and sorrows.

Fruit or Frustration

CHAPTER 10/Read John 15

A medical missionary dispensed pills to many of his patients. Imagine his amazement when he discovered that the pills were not being taken orally; they were fastened on a cord and worn around the neck as an amulet. After all, reasoned the patients, the pills' curative powers lasted much longer when draped from the neck than when consumed in the stomach.

Many people treat the gospel that way. Instead of "eating" the truth of the Word, they hang it outwardly for pious adornment. Their religion consists of outward adornment. Jesus was particularly harsh in His condemnation as He charged, "Woe unto you, scribes and Pharisees, hypocrites! for ye are like unto whited sepulchres, which indeed appear beautiful outward, but are within full of dead men's bones, and of all uncleanness. Even so ye also outwardly appear righteous unto men, but within ye are full of hypocrisy and iniquity" (Matthew 23:27,28).

Religion is an outward cloak to be worn at will. Christianity is an experience which changes the heart. "If any man be in Christ, he is a new creature: old things are passed away; behold, all things are become new" (2 Corinthians 5:17).

To receive Christ is to receive life. To continue receiving that life is to abide in Christ. He is the vine and we are the branches. Jesus appeals to us to seek the abiding life, to keep His commandments and abide in His love.

THE GENUINE VINE

Jesus makes His seventh and last declaration, "I am the vine," in John 15. His opening words are "I am the true vine."

The nation of Israel, referred to as a vine of God's planting (Psalm 80:8), failed to bring forth fruit for God (Hosea 10:1). As a result, the Lord set His face against His original vineyard and threw it open to the ravaging of the nations.

In the meantime, God the Father, as the Husbandman, planted a new Vine in the earth. That Vine is the Lord Jesus Christ, the eternal Son of God, who became incarnate in human flesh to provide redemption for lost mankind. All who believe on Him as their Saviour become members of His body, which is the Church, and become branches of the living Vine.

YOU GOTTA HAVE FRUIT

The new life which the disciples were to live after Jesus was gone is described in John 15 from three points of view: their relation to Christ (vv. 1-11); their relation to one another (vv. 12-17); their relation to the world (vv. 18-27).

Jesus, with His born-again followers as the branches, is the true Vine. The branches are many, yet they are all in the one body. That body is the one true Church of which Christ is the head. In Him the Church is enabled to fulfill the objective "to bring forth fruit." Fruit-bearing occurs both in the corporate activity of the Church and in each individual as a branch. Spiritual fruit-bearing is the normal result of this relationship.

The fruit of the vine is not produced by the branches, but it appears on the branches. A fruit-bearing branch is one which receives the lifegiving sap from the root without hindrance. Its secret is simply abiding.

Apart from spiritual fruit-bearing, a branch is worthless as far as adding any glory to the true Vine. Fruitfulness doesn't exist in mere activity but results from abiding.

A Part or Apart—Take Your Choice

The word *abide* is an expression used more often by John than any other writer in the New Testament. Of the 119 times the word appears in the King James Version, it is employed 67 times by John.

Why should John in his old age have used the word so frequently when writing about his Lord and the work of God? John was the youngest of all the disciples and outlived all the others. In his early years he had enjoyed the comfortable home of his father, who was a master fisherman with his own hired servants. In his later years, John suffered the loss of many things and was looking to his eternal home for an abiding place. Fully conscious of the transitory nature of the things of this earth, John saw that permanency lay only in eternal plans of God for His own.

"Abide in Me"

Jesus commanded us to abide in Him. We are in His hand, and we are to maintain communion with the Owner of the hand. Spiritual life is not static; it must grow. Continuous union is necessary. Jesus drove this point home with His solemn warning, "If a man abide not in me, he is cast forth as a branch, and is withered; and men gather them, and cast them into the fire, and they are burned" (v. 6).

These words teach the possibility of being connected with Christ yet later being severed from Him. This actually happened in the case of the branch. Does it occur in the case of a Christian? Those who hold the extreme teaching on grace will answer no. But we can't deny that the Bible teaches there is such a thing as an abortive experience.

When this happens, the cause lies with the disciple and not with the Master. If the Lord forsakes us it is because we have forsaken Him. We possess the ability to continue receiving the life of the vine or to shut off its lifegiving flow.

Take note of the progression of failure if we do not abide: unfruitful, withered, gathered, cast into the fire, burned. If we do not abide, we not only fail to bear fruit but also we no longer have life and, therefore, wither; and the end is eternal loss and final destruction.

ABIDE IN THE WORD

If faith is flagging, or if intellectual difficulties are looming too large, it may mean that prayer is being forgotten and the Bible is being left unread. We need to go beyond reading the Book. Jesus was saying, "Abide in me, remembering who I am."

WHAT IS LOVE LIKE?

Finally, Jesus said, "Abide in my love." This again is a command. We are to continue to live in such a way that the perfect flow of Christ's love into our lives will not be hindered.

The motivating power of all true Christian service is love (1 Corinthians 13). The ingredients of love are loyalty, obedience, vitality, enthusiasm. Love is more than a sentimental expression of emotionalism. Jesus always links love and obedience (v. 10). His commandments are not hard, harsh, or arbitrary for He is not an imperious slavedriver. His commandments, if obeyed, will bring only good to us.

Christ's love is not contingent upon our obedience. His love takes the initiative, but our realization of His love depends upon our keeping His commandments. Abiding in love is experiential. The love of the Father was a constant experience for Christ, because of His constant obedience. He invites us to a like relationship with himself.

In His love and mercy, Jesus commanded us to keep alive our spiritual life. The peril of many Christians lies right here. They neglect their spiritual life. Spiritual life must be nurtured, cultivated, watched. "Abide in me, in my Word, in my love."

THE PAYOFF

One of the results of abiding in Christ is an *effective prayer life*: "If ye abide in me, and my words abide in you, ye shall ask what ye will, and it shall be done unto you" (v. 7).

Another result is *continual* joy (v. 11). His joy, not ours. His joy is not dependent upon circumstances. When the lawyer tempted Him, Jesus "rejoicing in spirit, answered him." As He left the last Passover, Jesus knew that He was about to take the last few steps toward Calvary, and yet He sang the customary hymn of rejoicing (Mark 14:26). His joy is to "remain" in us—not here today, gone tomorrow. And our joy is to be full. His love is constant, but our experience and enjoyment of His love may fluctuate as we fail to abide in Him.

Still another result of abiding in Him is *fruitfulness* (v. 16). Three degrees of fruit-bearing are seen: "fruit" (v. 2), "more fruit" (v. 2), "much fruit" (v. 5). If there is no fruit whatever, the branch is taken away.

Fruit or Frustration

We are "in Christ Jesus," joined to Christ as a branch is joined to the tree.

God has placed the branch in a completely dependent position, since it receives all its life from the tree. Apart from the tree it has no life. If the tree fails, then the branch will wither and die. The Christian is in exactly the same dependent position. Apart from Christ's omnipotent power, and the life He imparts to us, we have no Christian life at all.

The basic helplessness of the Christian is declared by Jesus in plain terms, "As the branch cannot bear fruit of itself . . . no more can ye" (v. 4). The next verse is even more emphatic: "Without me ye can do nothing." Absolutely nothing! We are just helpless branches, completely and continuously dependent upon Jesus the Vine.

What a blow to our pride! We like to impress each other with our abilities and accomplishments, our knowledge and importance. But pride has no place in God's program. Self-effort is not in God's plan.

The Lord has to bring us to the place where we recognize our complete spiritual bankruptcy. Sometimes He has to employ rather painful means because of our obstinate ways. Our striving leaves only a trail of frustration and defeat.

STRENGTH FROM STRUGGLE

Jacob, the schemer, made this discovery (Genesis 32). After a night of wrestling with God, he ended up with his thigh out of joint. He left that struggle a cripple but vastly changed. No longer trusting his own skill and strategy, he learned to place his dependence on God.

Peter is so typical of us. He could do some of the greatest things, such as jumping ship to walk on the water to go to Jesus. Hear his bold declaration, "Thou art the Christ." Listen to his confident words, "Though I should die with thee, yet will I not deny thee." But see him a few hours later as with oaths and curses he denied three times that he had ever known Christ. He had to learn to not trust in his own strength. He was just a helpless branch.

Paul relates the struggle he went through in Romans 7 and 8. Listen to his experience. "For I know that in me (that is, in my flesh) dwelleth no good thing: for to will is present with me; but how to perform that which is good I find not. For the good that I would do I do not: but the evil which I would not, that I do" (Romans 7:18,19).

Looking helplessly to Christ, Paul finds the answer and shouts triumphantly, "There is therefore now no condemnation for those who are in Christ Jesus; for the Spirit's law life in Christ Jesus has set me free from the law of sin and death" (Romans 8:1,2, *Weymouth*).

ARE YOU STILL ALIVE?

The 1st, 3rd and 4th Rangers Battalions in World War II had a fearful casualty record. Fighting in the

Mediterranean theater of war, only 199 out of the original 1,500 men survived, and 64 of the survivors wore the Purple Heart. These rangers had an odd greeting when they met each other. It was, "Hello! How come you're still alive?"

We are only alive as we maintain our relationship with Christ. But the wonderful part about it all is that we don't have to struggle to maintain life. As the tree continuously and unfailingly gives its very inner life to the branch, so moment by moment Christ desires to impart His very own life to us.

The Christian life is nothing less than the continual flow of the very life of Christ himself within us. Take a concordance to find the many New Testament references to "Christ our life," "Christ in you," "abiding in Christ." We cannot read the New Testament without being made intensely aware that the essence of spiritual experience in apostolic times was the conscious awareness of the indwelling Person of Christ. In Him we have all things "that pertain unto life and godliness" (1 Peter 1:3). He dwells in our hearts and in our bodies which are the temples of God.

Putting It All Together

Jesus dosn't want to be our helper. He wants to be our *life*. He doesn't want us to work for Him; He wants us to let Him do *His work* through us. We can be the fingers on His hand! Fruit bearing is not produced by human effort; it comes through the unceasing flow of His life through our yielded personalities.

His life becomes our life (Galatians 2:20). We think as He thinks (Philippians 2:5; 2 Corinthians 10:5). We conduct ourselves as He would conduct himself (1 Corinthians 1:30). We overcome by the strength of His character (2 Corinthians 3:5; 1 John

4:4). His will becomes our will. We feel as He feels. Our ministry is Jesus himself ministering through us. He indwells us that He might commune with us, and we with Him (Revelation 3:20).

To abide then means: (1) to surrender wholly to Christ and accept our position as a helpless branch in the Vine; (2) to receive the inflow of the Vine's life; (3) to remain in intimate and close communion with the Vine.

Just as the flowing sap fills and swells the fruit, so the Holy Spirit, filling the surrendered life, encouraging, inspiring, restraining, rebuking, sharpening faculties, molding character, strengthening the mind and heart, and shaping the personality into the image of Him whose once it was, produces the only fruit which matters.

THE KAURI TREE

E. M. Blaiklock relates the following illustration of the inflowing of the Christ-life:

"At the rear of my property grows a kauri tree. The kauri vies with the redwoods in size and longevity. They have been known to measure 24 feet through and to be 3,000 years old. My largest kauri is a baby, some 300 years old and 11 feet around the base, a clean and beautiful tree. But all down one side, scarring some 10 feet of the bole, is a furrow of rotten wood. I once dug out some shreds of the dead wood, and looking closely at them decided they were not kauri. They were manuka, a much smaller tree, which grows in the first stages of a developing kauri forest, and dies out as the great trees take over.

"I at once saw what had happened. A manuka once grew beside my kauri. A century ago their trunks touched. In the years when your great-grandfathers watched Lee, and Grant, and Sherman, the blood of the kauri was flowing in white gum, and sealing the manuka to itself. Then with the passing decades the great tree sucked the life out of the smaller. Perhaps at the turn of the century the manuka died. The winter winds stripped its leaves and twigs. Bit by bit it fell away. Over seven years I have seen the healing of the scar. Blood still flows, but little by little the bark is returning. In 50 years nothing more than a groove in the trunk, and then that will fill. By A.D. 2,000 the mark will show only in the rings."

Our lives and Christ's met. We became new creatures in Him. He began to absorb all that was us and we grow into Him. Finally, we shall be found complete in Him. Forever He will bear the marks of the Cross in His body. He is the vine; we are the branches.

Love for One Another

The passage, verses 12-17, begins and ends with Jesus' comandment that we should love one another. Our love should be modeled after His love for us (13:34). His love is the greatest pattern (v. 13). Because of it, Jesus lifted the disciples from being servants to be His friends (vv. 14,15), and chose them to be His representatives in the world (v. 16).

Hatred From the World

The Gospel of John is filled with striking antitheses: belief and unbelief, light and darkness, life and death, love and hatred. In contrast with the Master's expressed love for us and the love we share one for another, Jesus fortifies us against the hatred which we will experience from the world (vv. 18-27).

With the forewarning that came to the disciples of the difficulties which were ahead, Jesus repeated His promise of the coming of the Comforter (vv. 26,27).

He's By Your Side

CHAPTER 11/Read John 16

In his autobiography *Years of Fulfillment,* Norman MacLean tells the story of an examination at the Coluton Parish School. One teacher had taught a class to repeat the Apostles' Creed, each pupil having his own portion to recite. The first boy began, "I believe in God the Father Almighty, Maker of heaven and earth." "I believe in Jesus Christ His only Son, our Lord," continued the second. The recitation went on to the boy who quoted, "He ascended into heaven, and sitteth on the right hand of God the Father Almighty; from thence He shall come to judge the quick and the dead."

A silence fell. After a few moments, one of the fellows piped up with these words to the examiner, "Please, sir, the boy who believes in the Holy Ghost is absent today."

Humorous? Yes, but that's close to the truth in many quarters. Those who believe in the Holy Ghost are scarce in many circles.

You Can't Program the Spirit

Many churches of our day are suffering chiefly

from the lack of the presence and power of the Holy Spirit. He is smothered in form and ceremony and affronted by unscriptural dogmas. Others are seeking to grow by employing gadgetry and a Madison Avenue sales pitch.

The Holy Spirit becomes a doctrine of a Presence without the *real* presence. The doctrine of the personality and power of the Holy Spirit may even be professed and even defended.

The liberals deny that the Holy Spirit is a sovereign person, while the orthodox affirm His sovereignty but do not want Him to act sovereignly.

All nominal Christian groups accept the Holy Spirit as long as He is loyal to their program. He must work peacefully within the framework they have provided and obey the rules they lay down.

But, thank God, He is pouring out His Spirit upon all flesh today in His divine sovereignty. While there have been outpourings of the Spirit through the centuries in a limited manner, the 20th century has seen the greatest outpouring of all time. The rain of the Spirit fell copiously at the beginning of this century, but it has been falling in an unprecedented manner in the last fifteen years.

Two Distinguishing Facts

This Christian age is marked by two great facts that distinguish it from every other period of time. First, there is a glorified Man in heaven. Second, there is a divine Person on earth. These facts are distinctive of the time period that began at Pentecost. The Man in heaven is the Lord Jesus Christ (Hebrews 10:12; Acts 13:38). The divine Person on earth is the Holy Spirit. Though He operated among men from Creation onward, He came in a new way fol-

lowing the glorification of Jesus to the right hand of
the Father.

GOOD NEWS ... BAD NEWS

The storm of the world's hostility was soon to
break with blazing fury upon the small band of disciples. The blind ignorance of organized religion
would actually cause men to believe that murder
was a service to God if it were done in the name of
religion.

Today, late in the 20th century, I've got good news,
and bad news! First, the bad news. These are angry,
confusing times in which we live. Tensions between
people and nations keep their teeth set on edge. The
family unit is breaking down. Permissiveness reigns.
Economic chaos causes men to throw up their hands
in despair. Inflation, depression, shortages in some
lines, other glutted! Bad news? Yes.

Now the good news. Jesus has the answers! He
did not leave His disciples alone when He left this
earth and has not left us alone today. True, Jesus was
about to leave the disciples, but Another was coming.
This other was the "Comforter." Whatever Jesus had
been, the Comforter was to be—and more.

John 14 told us that the Comforter would remain
(v. 16); the world could not receive Him or see Him
(v. 17), yet He would be with them; He would be
sent by the Father in the Son's name (v. 26); He
would teach the disciples all things and bring His
teachings to their remembrance (v. 26). And the
Comforter, the "Spirit of truth" (v. 17) would "testify of me" (John 15:26). In other words, the Holy
Spirit would reveal Christ's person and work. And
the Holy Spirit came to do for you exactly what He
came to do for the disciples.

Having referred to the coming of the Holy Spirit,

Jesus now goes on to explain more fully the nature of the Spirit's work. It was necessary for Jesus to depart from this world, that His work might be carried to completion by the Spirit.

How Loss Becomes Gain

No subject Jesus discussed with His disciples was less acceptable to them than His coming departure. They were emotionally unwilling to accept what He said (vv. 16-18). Both Peter (13:36) and Thomas (14:5) had asked questions in the Upper Room; but now when Jesus again referred to His departure, His words were received with stony silence (v. 5). The disciples were thinking only in terms of loss (v. 6), whereas Jesus wanted them to know that His going away would bring them great gain.

Jesus took time to prepare the disciples for the perilous days ahead by turning their thoughts to the spiritual comfort and strength which was to be theirs through the ministry of the Holy Spirit. This third member of the Holy Trinity had been at work since the beginning but had come and gone using various individuals as His instruments. He was now coming as the abiding presence to dwell in their hearts.

"It is expedient for you that I go away" (v. 7). One translation speaks of Jesus' going as an "advantage." Those disciples oppressed with a feeling of loneliness and weakness could not see their Lord's leaving them as an advantage.

How then did His going become an advantage? In the flesh Jesus could be in only one place at a time; in His ascended life He is omnipresent by the Spirit. During His earthly life He was external to men; by the Spirit He abides within our hearts. The grief of the disciples at the prospect of Christ's departure magnified an immediate need. Christ, on the other hand, saw down through the decades and centuries as His people, scattered by persecution, would know the blessing of an abiding presence independent of time and distance and an abiding power to witness to His saving grace.

THE SPIRIT DEALS WITH THE WORLD

Jesus proceeded to discuss the office and ministry of the Spirit; first, to the world, and second, to the Church. The Spirit's ministry to the Church is only a part of His assigned work. It is through Him that God also works in men's hearts to bring them to the knowledge of sin and the acceptance of salvation.

"He [the Spirit] will reprove the world." The word *reprove* may also be translated *convict* or *convince*. The Holy Spirit will convince and convict; He will arrest the world.

John used personal pronouns: "I . . . he . . . he . . . I" (vv.8-11), clearly identifying the person of the Spirit. He is more than an influence; He is acting on earth as the divine executive of the Triune Godhead. There is a difference between God as spirit and the Spirit of God. When we speak of God as spirit, we refer to His nature and substance (4:24). When we speak of the Holy Spirit, we refer to the Third Person of the Godhead.

The Holy Spirit takes truth—that which is morally right—and places it alongside the heart and life. Since truth can't be falsified, the sinner whose mind has been illuminated by the Spirit, at least to the degree of moral awareness, is made to see not only what is but what should be; and this in relation to his own moral condition. Thus he is reproved, convicted, convinced.

He Convicts of sin. Sin is a fact in human history. Sin is the root of all from which we suffer, yet the world knows little about sin as such. Oh, we have a lot to say about injustice, cruelty, dishonesty, and a hundred other things. But these are only symptoms. The deep, actual, and fundamental cause of all wrong is sin.

Jesus came to reveal God the Father, and by revealing Him, He revealed sin (15:22). God is righteous. As He is revealed to us, we see our own sinfulness. As dust on the furniture is not noticed in darkness, our sin goes unnoticed until the Holy Spirit brings us under the searchlight.

The sin that ultimately puts a person in hell is the sin of rejecting God's way out of hell. Therefore, in the final analysis, the sin question is related to our decision for or against Christ. The Spirit convicts men today not for having crucified the Saviour, but for not having accepted the crucified Saviour; not for the guilt of delivering Him up for death, but for refusing to believe in the One "who was delivered for our offenses, and was raised again for our justification" (Romans 4:25).

Unbelief is the root sin of the human heart (v. 9). Sin is not measured by relation to law; it is measured by relation to a Person, the Lord Jesus.

The first thing the Holy Spirit does is to convict of sin. He breaks down all the superficiality, the facade, the veneer of religiousness, of "devil-may-careness" which is put up as a front. He cuts through it all to make you feel and know what you really are. He will convict you of your sin.

He Convinces of Righteousness. Note the quick shift in the Spirit's approach when the first work—conviction of sin—is completed. Imagine you are seeing a great visual presentation. Lighting and color change with each new scene. The first has been portrayed under dark, somber light and backgrounds to bring out the deep, sordid, frightening aspects of sin. Then suddenly the light changes. The sordid fades into the distance. The picture changes from gloom to hope. Likewise the Holy Spirit introduces the bright light of hope. Righteousness has been made available.

Righteousness as an ideal comes into focus when the fact of sin is revealed. Sin came and righteousness was lost. Judgment was next. But between sin and Judgment came God-provided righteousness through the death of Christ on the cross.

The work of the Spirit here concerns the personal righteousness of Christ which would be proved beyond all shadow of doubt by His resurrection from the dead and His ascension to the right hand of the Father (vv. 7, 10). The giving of the Holy Spirit at Pentecost was a witness to the whole world of the validity of the Atonement and of the righteousness of Christ.

Our righteousness is assured for we are "accepted in the Beloved" and in no other way. Once you have confessed your sinfulness and have welcomed Christ into your life and believe that He died and rose again for your sake, and you trust Him personally, then the Spirit tells you very clearly on the authority of God's Word that *you are righteous* in God's sight.

He Convicts of Judgment. The final aspect of the Spirit's ministry in the world is to "convict" of judgment. This is not, as supposed by many, judgment to come. No one escapes the judgment of God. But the word here concerns the fact that the "prince of this world is judged" (v. 11; 12:31). Christ's atoning work defeated Satan. His hold over us is broken.

Martin Luther knew this and took his stand at Worms "though the devils be as numerous as the slates upon the housetops." John Knox knew this and dared defy Queen Mary of Scotland. History declares that "Bloody Mary" feared John Knox more than any army. And we too can live victoriously. "The prince of this world *is* [not shall be] *judged.*"

Following a rather famous prize fight, the winner was asked which blow won the fight for him. He replied that, while the bout ended in the 10th round, the knockout blow really was given in the 7th. From then on the loser was on the ropes awaiting the final knockout blow. Thank God, Jesus delivered the knockout blow to Satan at the open tomb. He's just hanging on the ropes and can't defeat us!

How the Spirit Provides

When Jesus said He would send a Comforter, He used the Greek word *parakletos*. It comes from two Greek words. *Para* means alongside. *Kaleo* means to call. *Paraclete,* therefore, means one called alongside. It can mean helper, advocate, intercessor, comforter.

In ancient tribunals it was the custom for parties to appear in court attended by one or more of their most influential friends, who were called in Greek, "paracletes," and in Latin, "advocatus." These gave their friends—not for fee or reward, but from love and interest—the advantage of their personal presence and the aid of their wise counsel. They advised them what to do, what to say, spoke for them, acted on their behalf, made the cause of their friends their own cause, stood by them and for them in their difficulties, dangers, and trials.

The spiritual presence of the Spirit necessitated the bodily absence of Christ. Jesus took humanity to God in order that the Spirit could bring divinity to man. Christ provides that which makes salvation possible; the Spirit performs that which has been made possible. Jesus supplies the resources necessary to Christian living; the Spirit applies those resources.

He Guides. My wife has an appreciation for the background of many fine pieces of music. She traces this back to a capable teacher in her grade school days. That teacher painted verbal pictures which opened to her students great vistas of music appreciation which enabled them to grasp the real meaning intended by the composer.

The Holy Spirit is the interpreter of Christ. He does not bestow a new or different revelation, but rather opens our minds to see the deeper meaning of Jesus' life and words. He will guide us "into all truth," but we must be on the move toward God before we can be guided. We can't be a stalled car.

Through His active agency we are preserved from error, receive divine illumination, and rightly divide the Word of truth. Observe that Jesus promised only to bring to remembrance "whatsoever I have said unto you"; that is, the things we have read and studied in His Word.

He Reveals. When the Holy Spirit comes, He not only guides us into all truth but He shows us things to come. Wherever you find people filled with the Holy Spirit, you find people looking for the coming of the Lord.

He Glorifies. The Spirit doesn't communicate the earthly Christ but the heavenly Christ, reinvested with His eternal power and reclothed with heavenly glory. Human language is totally inadequate to portray the personality of Christ because of His divinity. True knowledge of Him must come by revelation of the Holy Spirit.

The Calvary Road

CHAPTER 12/Read John 17-19

A restaurant operator had one consuming passion: to become a strong competitor of Howard Johnson's. He worked like a slave and became successful. But one day he was struck down with a terminal illness. The children were called home and stood with their mother around the dying man's bedside. They noticed his lips were moving. One of the sons stooped low to catch his father's last words. And this is what he heard: "Slice the ham thin."

That which possesses us in life will affect us in death. A dying request is likely to center about the thing nearest to the heart. If you have slaved all your life to create an estate, you will think of how it will be handled. If you have strong family ties, you will be thinking of those you leave behind. Christ had no estate to leave, but He did have those He loved and for whom He cherished the best. His greatest prayer included them.

The prayer which Jesus taught His disciples (Matthew 6:9-13) is customarily called the Lord's Prayer. Without arguing unnecessarily about terms, we would more properly call that prayer the Disciple's Prayer. The real Lord's prayer is John 17.

John 3 records our Saviour's greatest sermon; John

17 records His greatest prayer. Read it reverently, carefully, prayerfully, and repeatedly. Allow its spirit to capture you. Let its atmosphere penetrate into every part of your soul. Read it on your knees. Meditate on it. You will receive a new vision of the heart of Jesus.

A Glimpse Behind the Scenes

The great and matchless 17th chapter of John is the Sanctum Sanctorum, the holiest, of the Gospels. In chapter 9 reference was made to John 17 being comparable to the Holy of Holies of the tabernacle of the Old Testament. We are unable to fathom the depths of this sacred scene. We will know its heights only in that day when we shall know as we are known.

To share the true sense of the awesome scene of Christ in intercession before the Father causes us to remove our shoes, figuratively speaking, and to stand with bowed heads and hearts. We marvel at the majesty of it all—to have the curtain of eternity drawn aside and to hear God the Son in sacred conversation with God the Father.

The greatest battle of history was about to culminate. The Son was about to say, "O my Father, if it be possible, let this cup pass from me: nevertheless not as I will, but as thou wilt" (Matthew 26:39). His prayer was to be with "strong crying and tears," so strenuous that blood would ooze out of His pores with the sweat and fall in clots to the ground.

He prayed for us! Yes, He prayed for me! Could anything be more beautiful and encouraging. He who by example and action taught us loving service (John 13), and shared beautiful words of comfort and assurance (John 14-16), now prays. He prayed for himself, for His disciples, and for us (17:20).

The deathbed scene is very familiar to most ministers. I have stood again and again with families as their loved ones slipped into eternity. Some departures will forever be etched on my memory because of the stark horror of entering a lost eternity. Most have been beautiful because of the rejoicing with hope amidst the tears. I have listened as the one who has about run his course in this life has prayed and I became the better person for it.

Ask yourself the question, "If I were to pray a final prayer in this life, what would I pray for?" If I were uttering my last prayer, I'm sure that I'd be talking to God about the things I counted most precious and valuable.

Christ had deep compassion for all in their need, but He limited His high priestly prayer to three specific areas. He did not pray for the world, for the oppressed, for the sick.

First, He prayed for himself, not selfishly, but that His work might result in the Father's own glory and the good of all those who believe. He addresses God in the simplest and most intimate terms. Repeatedly He says, "Father"; once he says, "Holy Father" and again, "Righteous Father," and another time, "the only true God." Do we really understand and appreciate our privilege to come to God saying, "Our Father"?

As Jesus addresses the Father, He knows His "hour" has come, that God has given Him power over all flesh, and that He has finished the work He was given to do. He states that He has manifested the Father's Name and given the Father's words to the disciples, and has kept all but the son of perdition. This He

112

prays, being aware of the agony of Gethsemane and the indescribable suffering and humiliation of Calvary, which is just before Him.

The second part of His prayer is for His disciples. He petitions the Father to "keep them from the evil" and to "sanctify them" that they might behold His glory, share His presence and experience the Father's love.

How Can We Be One?

The third main portion of His intercession is for our spiritual unity—"that they may be one." It would seem that this was of utmost importance to Jesus, that His Body would have unity. The compelling reason was "that the world may believe that thou hast sent me" (v. 21). There is a unique oneness existing between God the Father and God the Son. They are one in essence, nature, and substance; and one in plan, purpose, and cooperation. Jesus prayed that we may be one even as He and the Father are one.

The unity of believers for which Jesus prayed is not achieved through the merger of church organizations. Jesus was speaking of an inner unity, effected by the Holy Spirit, transcending all external distinctions.

Satan's work is to divide the Church; Christ's work is to unify it. We should blush with shame when we allow minor matters to bring division among us. The harsh word, the divided vote on an issue, the heated exchange on policy—all these are the tools of Satan's work. Unity is of utmost importance. Disunity in the church causes disbelief in the world. Disunity is a sign of the Spirit's absence. The Holy Spirit came when "they were all in one accord."

Where Do You Fit?

Another significant expression in Jesus' prayer is

the oft-repeated word, *world.* He speaks of our being taken *out of the world* (v. 6) and yet, paradoxical as it seems, that we are *in the world* (v. 11). He indicates that we are *different than the world* (vv. 9,16) and *hated by the world* (v. 14). He doesn't pray that we should be *taken out of the world* but that we should be *kept from the evil* (v. 15). Then we come to the crux of the matter, the place of our relationship to the world. We are *"sent . . . into the world"* (v. 18).

Christ sends us in love. Who can measure the love that sent Christ from heaven's glory to Bethlehem's manger, to Gethsemane's battle, to Calvary's cruelty, and to the borrowed tomb? It beggars description. But that love wants to grip our hearts and motivate us.

David Garrick, perhaps one of the most famous Shakespearean actors of all time, went to hear George Whitefield preach. He tells how he pressed through the crowd until he was close to the preacher. A woman seated at Whitefield's feet cried out, "Sir, I have heard you preach five times since 7 o'clock this morning, and each time the scalding tears have flowed down your cheeks." Garrick, the great actor, went on to tell his friends how Whitefield preached until so overcome by emotion that he groaned aloud, "Oh! Oh! Oh!" "If only I could say 'Oh!' like George Whitefield," said Garrick, "I would be the greatest actor in the world." But that cry didn't come from Whitefield, for it was the cry of the Spirit (Romans 8:26,27), and it is born as we feel the love and passion of the Saviour.

As the Father sent the Son, the Son sends us that the world may believe, and know, and experience the love of God (vv. 21-23). *We are sent ones!*

114

Christ's agony of prayer in the Garden of Gethsemane, which is described in the Synoptic Gospels, is passed over by John, and the climax of His betrayal and arrest is rapidly reached.

WHEN SMALL MEN CAST LONG SHADOWS

The stillness of the night in the quiet garden was suddenly broken by the low sound of voices. Flickering torches and then a swinging lantern came into view. They were a nondescript crowd, little men casting long shadows, who were set on laying their hands on the most peaceable Person to ever walk upon this globe.

Out of the revolting scene stepped a familiar figure. It was Judas with a sickly smile on his face. With a kiss that must have scorched the cheek of our blessed Lord, he sold Him out for a few paltry pieces of silver.

The depth of the failure and disloyalty revealed in the act of Judas shocks us. But if we search our own wayward hearts we'll find the possibilities of a heart apart from the grace of God, for the "heart is deceitful . . . and desperately wicked: who can know it?"

One of the disciples in desperation cried out, "Lord, shall we smite with the sword?" Before an answer could be given, Peter pulled from the folds of his garment a sword and in reckless abandon struck out at the neck of the closest adversary. Fortunately, Malchus ducked and lost his right ear instead of his head. Jesus quickly commanded Peter to put away his sword and then gently touched Malchus' ear and healed him.

Peter took the way of the sword; Jesus chose the

way of the cross. Peter wanted revenge; Jesus brought reconciliation.

Jesus was seized by the motley band, manacled, and led away as a sheep to the slaughter.

Peter heard their bloodthirsty ravings fade in the distance, and as the last flickering torch disappeared among the trees the aloneness of it all engulfed him. They had taken his Master away, and the Master was walking into the jaws of death. Peter stumbled blindly along the path, following the mob at a distance, until he came to the palace of Annas. Flaming courage fled. Icy fear gripped the man who had gamely pulled out his sword.

WHEN THE ROOSTER PREACHED

A young girl identified Peter and asked, "Art not thou also one of this man's disciples?" In that moment the bombastic enthusiast found his heart turning to water as he denied his Lord: "I am not." Because the night was cold, a fire had been kindled, and Peter joined the group warming his hands at their fire. One of the soldiers caught Peter off guard with, "Art not thou also one of his disciples?" And Peter lied, "I am not." Finally with curses he denied the Lord a third time. And immediately the rooster crowed. Then Peter remembered! And the Lord had heard! Jesus turned and looked at Peter. A flood of memories raced through Peter's mind and his world came crashing. Hot, scalding tears poured down his cheeks and his rugged frame shook with sobs of remorse.

Jesus stood alone, deserted, before Caiaphas. His disciples had fled in confusion. Peter had even cursed Him. His face was marked from the blows of the cruel mob. His hands were bound. Now He was led before Pilate.

The cross-examination of Jesus by Pilate hinged on two questions. The first was instigated by Jesus' accusers and the second by Jesus' own statements.

The first, "Art thou a king?" exposes Pilate's weakness and the essential majesty of Christ. Jesus' reply was intended to uncover Pilate's source of information. Pilate was nettled by the implication that he had accepted hearsay evidence, though this was plainly evident.

The second question, "What is truth?" must have been an expression stated in helplessness, for Pilate went out to the assembled Jews and declared, not that Jesus was innocent, but that he could find no fault in him.

Pilate's maneuverings to avoid sentencing Jesus to death was not motivated by moral conviction but by fear and trembling. Jesus overawed Pilate, but the aggressiveness of the Lord's enemies cowed him, and he lacked the courage to render a clear-cut decision. Doubtless supposing that the mob would prefer Jesus to the nefarious Barabbas, Pilate gave them the choice, only to discover that to play loose and fast with justice is to play into the hands of men with evil designs.

HAVE YOU A WASH BASIN?

Matthew records that Pilate in the sight of all washed his hands saying, "I am innocent of the blood of this just person: see ye to it." Every city, town, and hamlet has a wash basin. Is there one in your church? in your home? Have you gone to the wash basin in an attempt to relieve yourself of the guilt of vacillation concerning Jesus? What have you done with Christ?

Barabbas was set free, stunned by the suddenness of it all.

From the distant courtyard there came the whine of the cruel scourge, into which had been fastened bits of glass and metal and bone and chain, ripping to ribbons the bared back of God's Son.

Jesus was stripped, spit upon, crowned with thorns, cruelly beaten, and led away to lonely Golgotha. He carried the heavy beam of the cross on His back, which was already raw and bleeding, cut to the bone by the thongs of the Roman scourge. Such floggings often produced death, but Jesus submitted to them for our healing (Isaiah 53:5). He suffered in our place.

There on the hill which is shaped like a skull was delivered the final ignominy. The nails were driven through blessed hands which had only reached out to comfort, heal, soothe, lift, and feed. The thud of the hammer was heard as the blessed feet, which had only walked to where people were in need, were pinned by great spikes to the cruel tree.

Mary's heart was almost wrenched from her. Peter was blinded with tears. Jesus' followers were stunned, horrified.

The soldiers took the crossbeam and lifted it upright. With each movement the nails tore the shredded flesh. Then with a sickening thud the cross was dropped into the hole in the ground.

The murder-crazed religious leaders had cried, "Away with him . . . crucify him!" Now they looked on Jesus hanging in agony and read the writing placed by Pilate, "JESUS OF NAZARETH THE KING OF THE JEWS." Pilate may have written in scorn, to bait those troublesome accusers of Jesus, but he wrote better than he knew when he designated Jesus as the Messiah.

Men made Calvary, and there they crucified the

118

Lord of glory. Between two thieves, He died for you and me. What a scene! The sinless Son of God, the hard and impenitent thief and the penitent one who found his way to Paradise in that hour. All the while there was the gaping, curious crowd and the hardened soldiers gambling for the Saviour's clothes. Some believe, and others turn away in callous unbelief. What a picture of the world today!

Mary stood there looking at her boy hanging alone and forsaken. With a tender, human touch, Jesus revealed His concern for her despite His agony by asking John to care for her.

Now we come to the greatest truth of all as Jesus cried out, "It is finished." This was not the despairing wail of a victim nor the faltering cry of defeat. It was the triumphant shout of the Victor!

The last drop of blood fell to the earth below. The world's greatest transfusion was provided. If talk of blood offends us, let us remember that crucifixion is a horrible, offensive death.

Maybe we need to be reminded that Christianity is more than poetry and song, flowers and stars, beautiful thoughts and good deeds. The Good News is more than the Christmas story and the Golden Rule.

The gospel deals with reality, with life as we know it. Our world isn't all prettiness; dreadful things mar it. But there was a cross and that hideous instrument of torture and death became the world's symbol of hope and deliverance.

Do Dead Men Stay Dead?

CHAPTER 13/Read John 20 and 21

Before me is a copy of the *Jerusalem Daily News*. The date is a Sunday, the year, A.D. 33. A startling headline covers the top of the front page, "NAZARENE'S TOMB FOUND EMPTY." Smaller headlines read: "Earthquake Rends City As Prophet Dies"; "Crucified King of the Jews Seen Alive Is Report"; "Body Stolen—Pilate."

The *Jerusalem Star* reports: "Body of Executed Leader Missing," stating, "Meanwhile, the police are searching for the whereabouts of the body in order to quiet the rumor once for all."

Can't you hear the newsboys of Jerusalem hawking their papers, "Read all about it! Grave's empty! Read all about it!"

Of course, it will not surprise you to find that these startling papers were printed only recently. They are attempts to bring the Easter story to life, to convey by contemporary journalism something of the excitement of the greatest story ever told.

Where is the Christian minister who has not wished he could find some way to excite people, to arrest their attention about the truth of the Resurrection. Are there words sufficient for the task? Yes, I believe there are. They are not new words; they are very old ones.

They are not written in a modern book but in one quite ancient. That Book is the New Testament. In a manner of speaking, that Book was the "Daily News." It wasn't called the "Daily News," but the "Good News." The Good News—the Gospel of the crucified, resurrected, ascended Christ—is the greatest news story of all history.

HAVE A NICE FOREVER

What is the great and lasting message which the resurrection of Christ brings to our hearts? Take the last two chapters of each of the four Gospels, and you have a series of the most intensely human stories in the whole of the Bible—stories of weeping women and the appearance of the risen Christ to them; stories of those who doubted and of those who were discouraged and Jesus' appearance to them.

The simplicity and certainty of the message is attested by the way in which it is told. Each appearance of Jesus—to Mary Magdalene, to Peter, to Thomas, to the Ten—answers to some definite human need.

Of all the stories pulsating with human interest, perhaps the most tender is that of Mary Magdalene. Very early on Sunday morning she told Peter and John that the body of Jesus, placed in the tomb on Friday, was no longer there. Her immediate reaction was to announce her conclusion that enemies had stolen Jesus' body. While Peter and John ran to the grave, examined the evidence, and returned to their homes, Mary returned to the tomb and stood outside crying. Looking in she saw two angels who asked her, "Why are you crying?"

Mary's tears were a sign of love. They were not the first tears she had shed for her Lord. She had been possessed of seven demons, and the Lord had delivered her. She had been forgiven much, and her heart overflowed with love. Now she had seen Him suffer such extreme pain at the hands of cruel soldiers and hateful men. When she found that His body was gone, she burst into uncontrolled tears.

Marys' tears were a sign of a lack of understanding. But before we condemn her, let's think of how we'd react. My parents and my wife's parents are buried side by side in adjoining family plots. Whenever we are privileged to return to our hometown, we visit the cemetery to check their graves and pause in loving memory. I can imagine my feelings if on the first visit I had found a gaping hole in the earth. Immediately I'd wonder where the thief had taken their bodies.

Mary was so conscious of her grief that she failed to recognize Jesus when He appeared to her in the garden. Many of us could learn a rich lesson from this. Mary turned back and saw Jesus within reach but didn't recognize Him. How often have you been so absorbed with yourself and your own ways to the point you fail to see Jesus.

Mary looked into the grave—Jesus was on the outside. Mary thought of death—Jesus was alive. Mary's thoughts were earthbound—Jesus was heavenbound. Mary's tears were unnecessary—Jesus wiped them away with His great big handkerchief when He spoke her name, "Mary."

Do Dead Men Stay Dead?

I guess the resurrection really boils down to the simple question, "Do dead men stay dead?"

This was the question Mary, Peter, and John faced.

The tomb was empty—there was no doubt about that. Three bleak, despair-filled days came to a climax for all of them with the discovery of the grave robbery.

To see Christ's resurrection with an understanding faith is a rewarding experience. Let's look candidly at the reactions of Mary and Peter and John.

Mary was the first one to the tomb. She represents the one-quick-look-is-enough attitude. Either too startled or too emotionally upset, she failed to realize the eternal significance of what she saw. Seeing the stone rolled away and the empty tomb, she ran to erroneously report the theft of Jesus' body.

Mary's error is common to many. They have scarcely so much as glanced at the evidence of the Resurrection. In the deep of every one of us is the big question of life here and hereafter. Life and death and afterwards are of vital importance. Yet many push it aside with only a casual look.

Two steps beyond the first casual look are needed to transform it into a satisfying faith. We understand the first by watching Peter at the tomb.

Some believe that John outran Peter to the tomb because he was a younger man. Maybe so, but isn't it possible that Peter ran with a heavy heart of bitter memories because of his miserable failures?

John paused outside while Peter became the first to enter the empty grave. Carefully he looked the entire situation over. His critical examination is expressed in the Greek word from which we get our English word *theory*. Peter tried to put together a theory that would stand upon all the known facts. He saw the linen clothes *lying*, not merely remaining on the floor, but lying precisely in the same position the body had occupied. There was the napkin, but *the head had been taken out of it.* Peter saw it all. Let's call it critical-seeing.

Finally John ventured into the tomb. The Bible tells us "he saw, and believed." From the Greek we get a rich meaning. It is the same as "I see it!" when you see through some baffling problem. John saw with his physical eyes exactly what the others saw. But for him the significance of what he saw was all that mattered. Before him were the unmistakable evidences of Resurrection—and he believed.

CONVINCING A DOUBTER

Thomas is an interesting person, so very human. The writer of the fourth Gospel had an obvious interest in Thomas. He presented him as a paradoxical person. In John 11:16, Thomas indicated his courage despite his pessimism when he said of Jesus, "Let us also go, that we may die with him." In 14:5 Thomas honestly admitted his lack of understanding of Jesus' words and, by his question, elicited a reply that has become one of our Lord's most quoted statements: "I am the way, the truth, and the life: no man cometh unto the Father, but by me." Here he is shown as a man hard to convince, yet enthusiastically responsive to irrefutable fact. Had he never missed church (v. 24), he would not have needed to doubt. You make a sad mistake by not attending church regularly. Absence from fellowship never helps us.

Doubt may come to any of us and in itself is not sin. It's a different matter when we cherish doubt and hold to it in unbelief. Don't make the mistake of doubting your beliefs and believing your doubts.

It's impossible for all of us to see; it is possible for us to believe (20:29). Faith that believes without the collateral evidence of sight is the faith that receives the fullest measure of reward.

124

From the introduction with its glorious climax: "We beheld his glory" (1:4) to the concluding confession of Thomas: "My Lord and my God" (20:28), we are driven to our knees in worship, for He is very God come in the flesh.

John presents the proofs of Jesus' claim to being the Messiah by selecting miracles and discourses from but 20 days in Jesus' three-year public ministry. None of the Gospels claims to be exhaustive; they were all selective. The Holy Spirit directed John to write as an eyewitness and close associate of Jesus. He was not to record the "many other signs" (20:30) but "these . . . that ye might believe that Jesus is the Christ, the Son of God; and that believing ye might have life through his name" (20:31).

The last chapter of the Gospel contains the story of another appearance of the risen Lord in which He directs words of instruction to seven of His disciples and then later to Peter specifically.

The disciples didn't know what they were to do. Peter was always a very active man. He couldn't stand to wait around any longer. He said, "I'm going fishing." The six with him said, "We'll go, too." They were fishermen when Jesus called them; now they were back at the old job. And their toiling was fruitless; they worked all night and caught nothing. In the morning Jesus was standing on the shore, but the seven didn't recognize Him. He told them to cast the net on the right side of the ship. Miraculously the catch was so great they were unable to pull it in.

This is our effort without God:
Human labor—Peter said, "I go a fishing."

Human influence—the other disciples responded, "We also go with thee."

Human failure—"that night they caught nothing."

But when God takes over:

Jesus' question—"Children, have ye any meat?"

Jesus' directive—"Cast the net on the right side."

Jesus' provision—"Now they were not able to draw for the multitude of fishes."

Dr. Alexander Maclaren comments: "It may be that we shall not see the results of our toil till the morning dawns and the great net is drawn to land by angel hands. But we may be sure that while we are toiling on the tossing sea, He watches from the shore, is interested in all our weary efforts. . . . Though we be on the tossing sea and He on the quiet shore, between us there is a true union and communion. His heart is with us, if our hearts be with Him, and from Him will pass over all strength, grace and blessing to us, if we only know His presence and owning our weaknesses, obey His command and expect His blessing."

BREAKFAST ON THE BEACH

When the disciples got their nets bulging with 153 fish on shore, they discovered that Jesus had prepared a good breakfast for them. After this expression of fellowship Jesus addressed himself to Peter.

Impulsive is the best word to describe Peter. He was no modest shrinking violet. Peter was at the head of every column and always talking. Whenever the apostles are listed, Peter's name is first. See him forsaking his fishing nets to follow Jesus and walking on the water at Jesus' bidding. Hear his great pronouncements: "Lord, to whom shall we go? . . . thou are that Christ, the Son of the living God"; "Thou shalt never wash my feet"; "I will lay down my life for thy sake."

126

Listen to Peter cursing fearfully as three times he denies his Lord. Feel for him as he weeps bitterly in shameful regret as Jesus looked at him. Peter never did anything by halves. There never was a gray area with him; it was either white or black, high noon or deep midnight. Strength or weakness, courage or cowardice, whatever it might be, it was always impulsive and intense.

The All-Important Question

Jesus asked, "Simon, son of Jona, lovest thou me more than these?" This is the heart of the matter. No amount of church activity or religious zeal, no apparent success in religious service, no position in the church makes this question unnecessary.

Three times Peter had denied His Lord. Now he is asked three times to declare his devotion to the Lord. Twice Jesus used a stronger word meaning devotion. Peter replies with a lesser word. The last time Jesus dropped to the lesser word Peter had used. This is what hurt Peter. "Do you even care for me?" That broke Peter's heart. He cried out, "Lord, You know all things; You know that I love you."

Peter had to learn that love—*love to Christ*—is the greatest thing. Neither conviction, confession, nor commitment can answer for simple, artless love. Lacking love, all would be lacking. Peter must know that love to Jesus is best shown by the disciple's relation to the flock of the Good Shepherd.

John calls love the greatest commandment (John 13:34). Peter calls love the greatest covering (1 Peter 4:8). Paul calls love the greatest constraint (2 Corinthians 5:14). Love cancels malice, smothers envy and consumes strife. Love begets hope, mothers peace, and

127

fosters joy. Love livest in the lofty heights of the heavenlies and the rarefied atmosphere of holy fellowship of that altitude kills the noxious weeds of self-seeking spirits of bickering divisions. Nothing is wanting where love rules the heart; everything is wanting where love is absent.

The supreme test of *life* is *love*. And the supreme test of *love* is *loyalty*. Peter had failed this test at the palace of the high priest. The same man whose spine buckled before a young woman's accusing finger faced a great crowd on the Day of Pentecost, preached with the unction of the Holy Spirit upon him, and won 3,000 converts to Christ. Without flinching, he faced persecution, trials, imprisonment, and (according to tradition) martyrdom.